This book is

Jesus who have a longing to be on the front line of God's kingdom.

May you be equipped and ready for the battle.

Please note:

All scripture references are quoted from the New American Standard Bible, unless otherwise stated.

This text updated and expanded March 2017

Contents

Preface

Ten or so years ago I published the first edition of Living on the Frontline, primarily for our church members at Frontline Church in Liverpool, UK. It was intended to be a simple introduction to spiritual warfare.

Since then I and the church have gone through some intense battles. More recently in my responsibilities in a regional network of churches, Together for the Harvest, and for a national network of churches, Kairos Connexion, I have become aware of a new urgency to see the church equipped for the battles that we are facing. In particular I saw a number of spiritual attacks taking place on key church leaders. These were intended to distract at best, or paralyse at worst those who are at the forefront of the missional movement in the UK.

As I talked to a number of those involved, I realised that there was widespread ignorance in the church about spiritual warfare, and a lack of knowledge of how to fight the battles at hand. It reminded me of the scripture in Judges 3:1-2 'These are the nations that the Lord left in the land to test those Israelites who had not experienced the wars of Canaan. He did this to teach warfare to generations of Israelites who had no experience in battle.' It seemed as though there was a whole new generation in church who had never been taught the principles of spiritual warfare, as many of us had been taught in the 1980's.

Battles may be sent by the enemy to bring damage and destruction to God's people. But God is able to help us turn those battles around into great learning experiences. Ones where we not only overcome the evil one, as we are intended to do, but also where we become equipped to win other battles and take more ground from the enemy. God is preparing his people for war once again.

I believe it is time to teach our churches the ways of warfare again, not only so we can be protected from the enemy's schemes, and defend ourselves when needed, but also so we can take kingdom territory as we prepare for Christ's return. If you wonder why we experience the battle or where it's all ending, then hang on to the end of the story. It's glorious.

This new edition has been fully revised with a number of new sections added. I pray it will be a blessing to you. 'Fight the good fight!'

1

Introduction

It was a relatively ordinary Sunday afternoon in November 1997 when the phone rang. I picked it up and heard my wife Jenny's voice for a brief second. Then all I could hear was the sound of emergency vehicles in the background before the call cut out - In a moment like that, every possible scenario goes through your mind. All I knew was that something awful had happened and Jenny was trying to contact me. I frantically tried to contact her but was unable to, so began the task of ringing the police to see if there had been an accident. Eventually, I was put through to someone who informed me that yes, Mrs Harding had been involved in an accident. They didn't know how serious it was, but thought they were on their way to Arrowe Park Hospital.

A week earlier, Jenny and I had been in Pensacola witnessing first-hand the revival scenes at the Brownsville Church. We had returned to the UK extremely excited and envisioned as to the impact this could have on our own church. On our return to Liverpool, we shared in the Sunday morning meeting. There was an amazing response from people and we had the opportunity to pray with many. It was on this same day that Jenny decided to go to the Ellesmere Port retail outlet with our two youngest daughters, aged 13 and 14, and one of their friends, who was 15.

As I raced to the hospital, I was filled with a strange calm (which can only have been the peace of God), but also a sense of apprehension as to what I would find. On arrival, I discovered that the car had been written-off, that Jenny and two of the girls had suffered whiplash and some bruising, but that one of my daughters was more seriously injured. X-rays eventually revealed that she had broken her spine and, because the fracture was right through the vertebrae, was in a potentially very serious situation where any movement of the bone could have caused paralysis.

After three weeks in hospital, a major spinal operation, and a further operation to remove some injured bowel, she finally came out of hospital sporting a full (but removable) body cast, and made her way towards total recovery. Thankfully, today she is able to do everything she wants to do and, apart from the occasional backache or muscle spasm, is symptom-free. (One small perk for her was that she did get to travel business class when she had to fly abroad for work. The guys who travelled with her were cooped up in economy quietly fuming!)

You are probably wondering what all this has got to do with spiritual warfare. Well, to understand the situation you need to know what was happening on a different continent at the same time...

In the hours building up to the accident Dave Connolly (my wonderful co-pastor) was in Richmond, Virginia, in the United States.

During the night, he had a horrendous nightmare in which he found himself battling with dark, demonic objects who were seeking to attack Jenny, our two youngest daughters and a third girl who he didn't recognise. After wrestling for what seemed like an eternity, he managed to subdue the opponents and they slunk off, but not before a final shot went over Dave's head. And he was unable to stop it. He woke up feeling exhausted, but, sensing the dream was significant, wrote it down immediately. He went back to sleep and twice more had the same dream with the same experience. When he woke in the morning and got to the church where he was preaching, he shared with the pastor there, who felt it was a warning sign, and decided that they should pray for our family. So there and then the whole church was asked to intercede for our family's protection, particularly for Jenny and the girls.

We can't be sure about the exact timings, but it seems likely that this prayer was taking place just moments before the accident happened. Minutes before the accident, Jenny had also suddenly felt prompted make sure the girls in the back were wearing their seatbelts.

Coincidence? I don't think so. I believe this was a severe attack from the enemy seeking to wipe out my family, probably in response to the new levels of faith and anointing we'd recently received, and were seeking to pass on to the church. At any rate, it is the most serious attack our family has ever experienced. The wonderful thing was that even though God allowed us to go through this experience, He was not standing back passively. He was working actively by sending a warning (through Dave) that the enemy was at work, and by engaging other Christians to intercede for us. I believe that without such intervention, one or more of my family would have undoubtedly been killed on that day.

What had happened was that an elderly couple had just returned from Canada and were badly jetlagged. They were driving along the A41, a section of dual carriageway without a central reservation on the Wirral. The wife (who was the passenger) dozed off first and was eventually followed by her husband, who fell asleep over the wheel due to his tiredness and jetlag. Their car swerved across the central reservation and straight into our oncoming car. There was no warning, no way the accident could have been avoided, and probably a total collision speed of around 80 miles per hour. The car was a complete write-off, with the front end totally caved in - What a miraculous escape! Thank God for his protection and for others sensitive to the Holy Spirit's warnings.

We need to be ready to take the battle to the enemy's gates and plunder his territory

I say all this not to frighten you, but to emphasise the reality of the spiritual battle in which we live and with which we must engage. We cannot bury our heads in the sand. As it says in 1 Peter 5:8, "Be self-controlled and alert. Your enemy the devil prowls around like a roaring lion looking for someone to devour." We need to be ready, not just to repel the enemy's attacks, but to take the battle to **his** gates and plunder **his** territory.

What is spiritual warfare?

Spiritual warfare stems from the reality that we live in a world dominated by two rival power structures. The first is the kingdom of God, which is victorious, advancing, taking more and more ground from the enemy, and seeing more and more lives transformed by His love and power. The second is the domain of darkness in which Satan seeks by various means to hold people in spiritual darkness, leading to death. He seeks to discourage, deceive, distract, defeat, damage or destroy those who have come in to God's kingdom of light.

...Imagine a man whose body has been infiltrated by a deadly virus. First of all, it begins to paralyse the nervous system, preventing communication from taking place within the body. Then muscle weakness starts to kick in, preventing him from walking or moving very far at all. After a while he starts to drift in and out of consciousness, unable to take control of his decisions or responsibility for his actions. As the end draws near, his whole immune system collapses and every other kind of virus and bacteria is able to invade his body. Cancers start springing up in all sorts of places, and ultimately he is destroyed by this infection. This is a picture of what the enemy wants to do to our lives. However, you have nothing to fear!

It would be a mistake to see this battle as two equal forces in which the outcome was uncertain. The Bible gives us a clear picture of the outcome in which Satan is ultimately defeated and destroyed in the lake of fire (Rev 20:10)[1]. There is no doubt about the outcome. We win! Satan's power and authority, although very real, are totally miniscule in comparison with God's power. God is the infinite, eternal, uncreated, all-knowing, omni-present, totally loving creator of the universe. Satan, by contrast, is a fallen angel (albeit one of considerable superiority). He is a created being with limited power who can only be in one place at a time and who doesn't know everything. There is no comparison. Imagine an ant trying to fight an elephant – no contest! *(Descriptions of how Satan fell are found in Isaiah 14:12-15 and Ezekiel 28:11-19. Revelation 12:7-9 suggests that demons are other angels who rebelled with Satan, one third of the total[2])*

So, although we have nothing to fear, we do need a healthy respect for and awareness of the devil and his strategies. This is a war that we ultimately win, but there are battlefield casualties along the way. Not every skirmish ends in our favour, but the wonderful thing is that God works all things together for good, even when the enemy seems to have defeated us in a particular situation. When we hand that situation back to God, He will always be able to bring something good out of it.

When the children of Israel had left the promised land, it says in Judges 3:1-2 that the Lord left some of their enemies in the land in order "to test them so that the generations following might be taught how to wage war." This is a great picture of the situation we are in now. The enemy still stands as an illegal squatter on God's planet. Under his authority Satan has many demonic powers and evil spirits. God expects us to learn how to wage war and not be victim to their strategies. God intends for us to be strong, alert and victorious. A child that is spoiled and given everything he or she wants grows up without character or backbone. But when they have to fight a few battles along the way, they become people of strength and compassion.

We can fall into two common deceptions when it comes to the demonic realm: We can either see a demon behind every tree and become focused on Satan instead of Jesus; or we can choose to believe that the devil doesn't exist or that he is not relevant to our lives, in which case we are unwittingly subject to his deception and lies. We need a healthy balance that keeps our lives focused on Jesus, but aware of the enemy's schemes (2 Cor 2:11[3]).

2

The basis of our victory

If someone told you that you were going into a fight that you were guaranteed to win, you would want to know how that was going to happen before you ventured in to the ring. It is not unreasonable for us to want to know on what basis we can claim victory in our warfare against the enemy.

Since the beginning of creation, when the devil appeared in the form of a serpent to Adam and Eve, he has been active and seeks to destroy our lives, hinder God's work, and spoil His kingdom. The promise of victory is found right back there in Genesis 3. Once Adam and Eve have confessed what happened, God says to the serpent, "I will put enmity between you (Satan) and the woman and between your seed and her seed. He shall bruise you on the head and you shall bruise him on the heel" (Gen 3:15).

This reference to the seed of the woman is referring to Jesus, who we are told will crush Satan on the head even though he (Satan) would attack His heel. It's clearly a reference to Christ being crucified. Christ was not just bruised of course, but horribly tortured and crucified. However, at a much greater level, the devil himself was totally defeated on that day.

We can apply the same picture to the church as the seed of the woman, living in the authority and victory of Christ. Satan may find our Achilles' heel from time to time, but the outcome is certain. We can, must, and will crush him under our feet.

This picture is again picked up in Psalm 68:21-23: "Surely God will shatter the head of His enemies ... Your foot may shatter them in blood." Psalm 91:13 says, "You will tread on the lion and the cobra. The young lion and the serpent you will trample down." In Psalm 108, again God is seen to be treading His enemies under His feet. And in the New Testament the same sentiment comes through in Romans 16:20 when it says, "The God of peace will soon crush Satan under your feet" (i.e. the feet of the church). It gives new meaning to the scripture in Joshua 1:3 where God says, "every place where the sole of your foot treads, I have given it to you." Through these scriptures we see that it is the working together of Jesus and His church that ultimately delivers the deathblow.

> *It is the working together of Jesus and His church that ultimately delivers the deathblow*

The cross of course is where the real action takes place. Colossians 2:14-15: "Having cancelled out the certificate of debt (the penalty of our sin), He has taken it out of the way, having nailed it to the cross. When He had disarmed the rulers and authorities, He made a public display of them, having triumphed over them through the cross." Satan thought the cross was his finest hour, like the White Witch in CS Lewis' *The Lion, the Witch and the Wardrobe.* She revelled in Aslan's death and defeat, not realising the 'deeper magic' that was at work, which would ultimately result in her own destruction and Aslan's victory. (If you haven't seen the film or read the book, you really should!)

As Jesus hung on the cross, taking the punishment we deserved, bearing our guilt and shame, carrying our sicknesses and emotional pain (Is 53:4-5[4]), all the things the enemy uses to trap us were taken out of his hand. When Jesus rose from the dead, defeating death itself, Satan's ultimate threat over us was also removed and the fear of death could no longer hold us. Hebrews 2:14 says, "Jesus took on flesh and blood that through death He might render powerless him who had the power of death, that is the devil, and might deliver those who through fear of death were subject to slavery all their lives." What an amazing day of defeat for Satan. What a great day of rejoicing for God's people, the church!

Walking in that victory is not automatic. We have to truly know and understand that Satan has been defeated. Otherwise, he will use deceit to trick us into believing that we remain

21

subject to him. As long as he can get us to believe that, then we are trapped. Once we understand, declare, and walk in the good of that victory, the victory that Christ won for us, he is rendered powerless and the fear of death is destroyed. For each one of us death is not the end but the doorway into a fuller experience of the eternal life we receive at salvation. Destruction and death came through Satan, but eternal and abundant life has come through Christ (John 10:10[5]).

Is he totally destroyed? No he is not. He is defeated, but not yet destroyed. That destruction is waiting for the day of Christ's return and the final judgement when Satan is cast into the lake of fire (Rev 20:14[6]). In the meantime, we live in a period that is similar to the interval between D-day and VE-day in the Second World War. On D-day (the day of the Normandy landings), the enemy suffered a mortal blow from which he could never recover, but he still continued to fight and cause many more casualties. However, it was only a matter of time before the Allied troops were able to advance into the heart of Germany itself and Hitler's reign was finally ended for good. VE-day (Victory in Europe day) finally hailed the end of the war. For us, that promised day is coming, but for now we are still living in war-time.

For this reason, we do not expect to get through the battle unscathed. We are waging a real war, but it is with a defeated enemy. Sometimes a wounded animal can be at its most vicious when it senses its end is near. So we don't take the enemy lightly, but neither do we fear him.

In the meantime, we stand with Jesus in His commitment to destroy all the devil's works; to liberate those who are caught in the traps of sin and addiction; to bring light to those who are in darkness; to bring good news to those who see nothing but hopelessness; to bring joy to families and communities; and to bring about the transformation of our towns and cities.

"The son of God appeared for this purpose that He might destroy all the works of the devil"

1 John 3:8 says that "the son of God appeared for this purpose, that He might destroy the works of the devil." What a joy to see the enemy flee as the word of God promises us! (James 4:7[7]) We can say with the apostle Paul, "through Christ we overwhelmingly conquer" (Rom 8:37) and, "thanks be to God who gives us the victory through our Lord Jesus Christ. Therefore my beloved brethren, be steadfast, immovable, and always abounding in the work of the Lord, knowing that your toil is not in vain" (1 Cor 15:57-58).

3

Primary arenas of warfare

ARENA 1 - The mind

One of the first areas the devil will seek to capture is our mind. He knows that if he can establish a lie or a stronghold in our mind, then he can have control over certain attitudes, words, behaviour and even actions.

When a military coup takes place in a country, the first targets are radio stations, TV stations, government offices, air traffic controls, and border crossings - In other words, all the centres of communication and control. So, it is not surprising that the devil targets the human mind! After all, "as a man thinks within himself so he is." (Prov 23:7)

We are told in John 8:44 that the "devil is the father of lies and has lied from the beginning."

If a lie can be sufficiently established in our lives, we end up deceived by "the deceiver" (another name for the devil - Rev 12:9). You don't have to have gone into a cult or into gross immorality to be deceived. If the enemy convinces me that I am ugly or worthless, then I am living in deception and am restricted from fulfilling God's call on my life, for which I need confidence and a true value of myself.

The mind is also the place where temptation first takes place. Temptation always begins with an idea. It's an idea that appeals to our fleshly nature. If we have not crucified our flesh through identifying with Christ's death and resurrection, the flesh is always ready to latch on to a tempting idea that the devil puts in our mind. For example:

- "There's no need to tell the shopkeeper that he's given you more change than you needed"

- "One of the girls in my office seems to think I'm quite smart. Perhaps I should take her out for lunch."

- "I really ought to buy that new dress. It will make me happy."

- "If I call in sick today, I could make a long weekend of it."

...so the list goes on. Temptations range from the small and simple things to the complex and potentially life threatening. We know that God does not tempt us[8] (James 1:13), but we know that the devil does[9] (1 Cor 7:5). Just as Edmund in *The Lion, the Witch and the Wardrobe* was tempted by the White Witch with the Turkish delight, we are often tempted by things which appear irresistible to us.

And when we give in to temptation sufficiently often, we develop a pattern of behaviour. In other words, the enemy gains a strong hold on part of our lives, because we have repeatedly given in to a particular temptation and the sin that follows. A man who repeatedly gives in to sexual fantasy and the use of pornography, for example, eventually becomes trapped by it. A stronghold is established in his life, and an addictive behaviour pattern is the result. In 2 Corinthians 10:4-5[10], Paul likens these strongholds to fortresses that need to be pulled down stone by stone. Each one of these powerfully reinforced areas of enemy stronghold is set up by him to oppose a true knowledge of, love for, and relationship with God. But the promise in this scripture is that God gives us the weapons to deal with them *(see chapter 4 – the weapons of our warfare)*.

> *Strongholds are hard work to demolish, but this is battle that everyone*

Ed Silvoso says that a stronghold 'is a mind-set impregnated with hopelessness, that causes us to accept as unchangeable situations that we know are contrary to the will of God.' We must recognise them for what they are and not give into hopelessness, we must fight with all the weapons at our disposal.

Have you ever had those thoughts come into your mind that seem to accuse you, condemn you, or generally make you feel unacceptable and worthless? These are the accusations of the enemy (Rev 12:10[11]). He often tries to convince us that we are not forgiven or even that we have committed the unforgivable sin. I've had many people come to me over the years believing they must have committed the unforgivable sin. Anyone who's concerned they may have committed the unforgivable sin certainly hasn't. To have defiled the Holy Spirit and be so alienated from God that it would be impossible to return to Him would mean the individual would certainly not be concerned about whether or not they had committed the unforgivable sin! The very fact of their concern means they cannot have committed it. God is ready to forgive anyone who comes to him with a repentant heart, no matter what they have done.

The enemy always uses the same old tactics of deception and accusation. He will accuse us of not being good enough, not praying enough, not being loving enough towards our spouse or family, and so on. We do of course need to recognise when the Holy Spirit convicts us of these things, but there is a very big difference between condemnation and conviction!

Conviction leads to clear repentance from which we gain peace with God and a sense of relief. Condemnation, on the other hand, simply makes us worry about the issue concerned and leaves us feeling there is no way out from it. It's as if we are standing in quicksand and the harder we try to get out, the more we sink. Conviction is clean, clear, and releasing. Condemnation is unclear and confusing. Condemnation locks us up, paralysing us from further action and making us believe we have no place in relating to God. It is vital therefore that we identify the condemning accusations of the enemy clearly and deal with them appropriately.

It's interesting to note that some peoples' consciences can become quite dulled to conviction because of lifetime habits of sin. Others are over-sensitive and fall prey to condemnation and accusation. Ask your best friend which of the two traps you are more likely to fall in.

Some years ago, I was in a meeting in the United States. Completely unrelated to the ministry that was taking place, the Holy Spirit highlighted an issue in my life - a stronghold of self-hatred. I had been completely unaware of it up until that time, but as He put his finger on it, I realised that I had always seen myself as inferior because I was vertically challenged (short). As people prayed for me on that day, I was completely set free from that stronghold and I have never succumbed to it again. I may be short on the outside, but inside I am a giant! Although this was rooted in a false belief (a lie), it also had an emotional component, which we will go on to look at next.

ARENA 2 - The emotions

The emotions are closely linked to the mind. Many of the areas where we become locked up or oppressed emotionally start off with an attack to the mind. Fear and anxiety, for example, start off with an innocent thought that usually begins with 'what if'. Using our imagination, we quickly start to think of all the possible negative things that could take place. We see ourselves getting into debt, getting sick, failing an exam, losing a relationship, not being promoted, crashing our car etc. These thoughts are particularly powerful in affecting our emotions if they involve situations that we are powerless to do anything about. For example, whether I am promoted or not is entirely in the hands of my employer. Ultimately, there is nothing I can do about it except do my job to the best of my ability.

Depression can often be a follow-on from prolonged anxiety. The book of Proverbs tells us that "anxiety in a person's heart weighs it down" (Prov 12:25). As a GP I used to see many depressed people who could not really identify any clear reason for their depression. On further questioning, it became clear that for years they had been chronic worriers. It was almost as if they had used up all their nervous energy body chemicals and now had nothing left. The emotional cupboard was bare.

In Matthew 6:14-15[12], Jesus said our being forgiven by God is dependent on us forgiving others. It's almost as if our 'forgiveness-receptors' are blocked by our own unforgiveness, leaving us in the grip of anger, resentment and self-pity. In Ephesians 4:26-27[13], Paul explains very clearly that when we fail to forgive we give the devil an opportunity to gain a foothold in our life. These emotions block out our ability to experience the love and forgiveness of God (for ourselves) and lead to all sorts of destructive compensating behaviours, leaving us feeling pretty unhappy about life. Often these emotions are generated by painful experiences in our childhood when, through no fault of our own, we have been exposed to damaging situations. The enemy takes full opportunity. He has no respect for a person and certainly no respect of age. If he can distort our thinking and lock up our emotions from childhood, then he has lots to twist, manipulate and play with when we reach adulthood. Getting free in these areas is a major act of spiritual warfare. I recommend 'Forgive, Release and be Free' by Joff Day for any who need to work through forgiveness issues in a thorough and systematic way.

Feeling guilty and ashamed is often linked to the condemning lies of the enemy. With such a loss of self-esteem, we rarely feel qualified, able, or invited to take part in serving God and seeing Him work through our lives. For example, a woman who has had an abortion may still feel condemned about what she has done even if it was years ago. She feels unclean, unworthy, excluded and rejected. She needs to experience God's forgiveness and self-forgiveness to be fully set free. Otherwise, the enemy scores again.

ARENA 3 - The will

Again linked to the mind, the enemy plants doubts in our thinking which leads to double-mindedness. We find ourselves unable to make a decision, analysing things from every which way - We end up with 'analysis paralysis'. James 1:6-8[14] tells us that such "a double-minded man is unstable in all his ways." Double-mindedness leads to instability of character and we become unable to trust or be trusted. Imagine a fearful driver approaching a busy intersection. They sit waiting for ages for a gap in the traffic. Finally, they spot one and start to tentatively move out. They think they see something move out of the corner of their eye and slam on the brakes, thinking they have failed to see an oncoming car. Realising this is not the case, they panic because they have now stopped halfway across the road. They reverse, they go forward - by which time traffic has arrived and they are stuck in the middle of the junction, a danger to themselves and a danger to others. Similarly, the enemy is able to paralyse us and bring us into a place of inactivity through confusion and double-mindedness, because we become unable to make decisions.

Others are simply weak-willed. They lack resolve. They are unable to make decisions to do things because the enemy has worn them down through discouragements, disappointments and feelings of failure over their past attempts to do things. Or perhaps they have always had people do things for them, so have not needed to take responsibility and make their own decisions. The enemy is very happy to keep people in this weakened state where they lack the will to act. Self-discipline becomes almost impossible and they resort to the easy options of feeding the flesh and looking for the comfort and stimulus of activities that cost them nothing.

At the end of the day, our wills need to be completely in line with God's. They need to be strong and able to make decisions even in difficult circumstances. Moments before He was arrested, even though He knew what was going to take place and all the pain and suffering He would endure, Jesus still prayed, "not my will, but yours be done" (Luke 22:42). We need to have that same obedient heart to our heavenly father. Our wills need to be clear and focused on God's plan for our lives. And they need to be able to overcome the fleshly desires for self-indulgence and comfort through the appetites. Profound repentance is nearly always required.

"Choose for yourself today whom you will serve" – make a clear decision

Joshua 24:15

The most fundamental of all choices is the choice to follow God and to follow Him fully. Joshua put it this way: "Choose for yourself today whom you will serve... but as for me and my house we will serve the Lord" (Joshua 24:15). Joshua made a clear decision. He was going to lead by example. It's an example we would do well to follow.

We may need the help of others to whom we can make ourselves accountable to strengthen our will. In other words, when we make a decision to strengthen our will, overcome a sin issue in our lives, or put to death a fleshly appetite, it can help to share it with someone. Asking a close friend or leader to ask us regularly how we are doing in a certain area can be huge help. We may need their encouragement to strengthen our wills, but strengthen them we must! After all, spiritual battles take captive the weak-willed (2 Timothy 3:6)[15].

ARENA 4 – The physical body

Time and time again in scripture, we see physical sickness related to enemy activity. While some sickness seems to simply be a result of the fact that we live in a fallen world with disease and decay all around us, it is clear from the gospels that Jesus linked sickness on many occasions to enemy activity. Indeed, casting out the demon would often cause the sickness to be completely healed. It says of Jesus in Acts 10:38: "You know of Jesus of Nazareth, how God anointed Him with the Holy Spirit and with power, and how He went about doing good and healing all who were oppressed by the devil, for God was with Him."

Sickness can immobilise us, putting us out of action and rendering us ineffective in serving God. It can cause us to be depressed and even suicidal where chronic pain gnaws away at the will to live. Sickness can also take up much of our time and the time of others who are involved in caring for us. Whilst God can use periods of sickness to work on our character and to allow others around us the privilege of supporting and serving us, this is not the norm. We need to learn to fight sickness, seeing the hand of the enemy behind it.

I have a had to learn to do this in my own life. After 20 years of suffering with debilitating headaches three to four times per week, I finally got the breakthrough in the Easter of 2006. Jenny used to get so frustrated by these headaches because they robbed me and us of so much quality time together. They would push me into my 'coping cave', communications would shut down, and socialising would be right off the agenda (it was never that high to start with!)

Eventually God showed me that I needed to engage in the battle and fight against these headaches. I started waging war on them by praying on a daily basis to break the power of a spirit of generational migraine off my life, and to forbid headache (my mum and grandma both suffered with migraine). After consuming between six and ten strong painkillers each week, since Easter 2006, I did not need to use any for many years. Praise the Lord!

I have had odd seasons of headaches since, but generally if they start to build up I need to resist them, being very careful not be become dependant

I determined to be a victim no longer and to start taking control of my health in Jesus' mighty name

on painkillers again. I drink plenty of water and expect them to go. Most of the time they clear without painkillers. It has transformed my life. I determined to be a victim no longer and to start taking control of my health in Jesus' mighty name. God gave me the revelation of how to pray and the enemy's hold was broken. I still pray daily, as I know I have to remain dependant on God for my healing.

After seeing a consultant I was told I probably had prostate cancer. It hit me like a sledgehammer. I remember sitting in the consulting room in a daze. I had not been expecting it at all. The next 3 weeks were a constant battle, both for my health, and to overcome the fear that was lurking constantly in the shadows. After all the tests were completed the conclusion was that I didn't have cancer. Praise God. We have to battle for peace of mind when sickness comes to rob us of it.

As a regular practice, I have for about 20 years or more, spent time each morning, usually in the shower, making declarations of health, and rebuking sicknesses by name, forbidding them to come near me or my family. I find this vital to remain in a place of faith for good health. They say that prevention is better than cure, and I think that resonates not only in the natural but also the spiritual. Clearly staying fit and eating well is also massively important.

I think by God's grace I have probably taken less than one day off sick every 2 years. I don't take my health for granted, but continue to trust God for it so that I can serve him till the day he takes me home!

Our daughter's accident that I spoke about earlier was clearly the result of a highly orchestrated demonic strategy to wipe out my family. That accident was no coincidence. The enemy set up the circumstances to bring it about. Some people find themselves accident-prone. This may even run in families and be an inroad that the enemy has established through the sin of past generations. We must remain alert and prayerful, cutting off these ties, and looking out for fresh attempts the devil may make to disable us through accident or injury.

Ultimately the enemy wants to steal, kill and destroy. But Jesus came that we should have 'life in all its fullness'. We know that the body eventually decays and we die. We don't need ti beat ourselves up when we see signs of waging, but many people are old before their time.

ARENA 5 – The family

The marriage relationship is ordained by God,

and Genesis 2 shows the importance of that relationship as we seek to serve God. In fact, in Genesis 1:28, God's command to "be fruitful, multiply, fill the Earth, subdue it and rule over it" was given to man and woman together. Clearly, if the enemy can sabotage this most crucial of all relationships, then both husband and wife will feel disqualified from serving God and from being effective in his kingdom. The break-up of a marriage is always a tragic thing and so often we see the enemy's hand at work, from small things like little misunderstandings to big things like one or other partner being tempted to engage in an adulterous relationship.

Sadly, Jenny and I have seen a pattern repeated time and time again. It starts with a little disillusionment with the church (with the leaders or in other relationships). It gradually leads to offence and withdrawal. Eventually, the couple leave the church with a variety of justifications and excuses – usually blaming the church leaders or others who have 'hurt' them. Within a year or two of being out of fellowship, their relationship with God starts to disintegrate. The enemy has such a strong foothold through that offence that the couple start to blame God for everything that has gone wrong.

With the protection of the church gone and God's presence lifting from them, they are prey to every temptation. The moral code they previously lived by no longer seems relevant. Biblical absolutes are questioned and soon the couple (usually one before the other) start to look elsewhere for happiness. The marriage is doomed by this stage and it's not long before they are just another divorce statistic. Tragically, Satan wins again.

Any kind of abuse in the home or just plain old laziness and selfishness can quickly erode what was once a vibrant and dynamic relationship. Again, unforgiveness gives room for the devil in this situation and pride - the original sin of the devil - will cause either or both partners to refuse to say sorry or admit their fault, thus escalating the damage to the relationship.

Debt can be a crippling factor to many

marriages and families. And I believe this temptation to live beyond our means and incur spiralling debts is in fact another demonic strategy, fuelled by temptation through advertising and materialism.

With so much pornography available at the newsagents, on the TV and on the Internet, the temptation to unfaithfulness is like an underground stream eroding the foundations of a building. Before we bought our present house, there had been some subsidence to one corner of the building simply because a drainpipe had been allowed to leak into the soil by that corner. Because it was built on sandy sub-soil, that sand gradually got washed away and the corner of the house started to move. Similarly, the constant dripping of sexual temptation, particularly for men, undermines marriage and often leads to unfaithfulness. Trust is very hard to regain after such an experience and many marriages will fall apart.

Not only is the testimony of a broken marriage a shameful thing to a husband and wife, but the fallout for the partners and any children leaves its scars for many years to come. Once again, the enemy has scored.

Children who grow up without one or either parent are at a clear disadvantage. It may not be politically correct to say so, but children need a mother and a father. And whilst some children grow up remarkably unscathed in single-parent families and many single parents do a fantastic job of raising their kids, that is not God's intention. It is a strategy of the enemy to deprive youngsters of the security and balanced input that they need from a mother and a father figure, with marriage providing the stable basis for that relationship.

Children who are not raised with any respect for authority, parents or elders will generally grow up to be rebellious. Children without boundaries become the centre of their own lives and can cause great destruction within their families and in the local community - We often don't have to look very far beyond our own front doors to see children running wild.

The spirit of lawlessness, which characterises the end times, does seem to be increasing in our culture (2 Thes 2:3-7)[16].

Screen time – TV, the internet, and computer games consume a huge amount of our time, wasting great opportunities for investing in things of eternal value. Whilst a certain amount of screen time can be relaxing or even educational and faith building, the sheer quantity, let alone the poor quality of it is a huge distraction at best, and soul pollution at worst.

In 2017 the BBC reported that the average child (5-16 yrs old) spent 6.5 hours per day on screens

In 2017 the BBC reported that the average child (5-16 yrs old spent 6.5 hours per day on screens, rising to 8 hrs a day for teenage boys*. I have to admire those who have made the decision not to have a TV or to strictly limit screen time in order to protect their children's time and their minds.

The enemy will do all he can to destroy family life. He knows it is the bedrock of any healthy society, and that the extended family is the primary unit of the kingdom of God

ARENA 6 – The church

If you ever wanted evidence of the devil at work, just look at the number of church splits, burnt-out church pastors, feuding deacons, dead religious institutions, and manipulative and controlling teachings in our churches.

Fortunately, we have the promise from Jesus that it is He who is building His church, and the gates of hell will ultimately not prevail against it. In the meantime, they seem to be doing a pretty good job. Our starting point, however, is the victory that Jesus proclaims for the church and what we know of its outcome in the book of Revelation as "a bride adorned for her husband" (Rev 21:2).

The church has the greatest potential to destroy the powers of darkness because of its unity and the release and flow of spiritual authority, not to mention the sheer power of numbers praying, loving, and evangelising.

There is also the capacity for a corporate anointing of the Holy Spirit, which can break through strongholds of the enemy that cannot be tackled on a purely individual level. The

> *The church has the greatest potential to destroy all the powers of darkness because of its unity, and the release of spiritual authority*

church is the greatest war machine that God has ever invented, but we need to know how to protect it, nurture it and release it onto the battlefield so that it does not get bogged down in the quicksands of confusion, competition, compromise, or control.

Probably the breakdown of relationships within the church is one of the enemy's biggest strategies. He seeks to create breakdowns in many areas, such as communication, misunderstandings, false comparisons, jealousies, stupid squabbles, and differences of opinion (everyone seems to have an opinion about what should happen in church). And then with a lack of grace, forgiveness and humility, the divide opens up. Satan is well-versed in the principle of dividing and ruling. And Jesus even recognised and warned us of how destructive this could be (Mark 3:24-25[17]).

This all means that we must be vigilant to avoid gossip, negative talk, criticism, back-biting, and rumour-mongering, and instead be honouring and respectful in the way we speak of each person and especially of those in leadership. The enemy wants us to take offence and will set us up in situations where through misunderstanding or human failure, taking offence seems like the easy option. Instead we must deal with our own response to the situation, first through repentance and then by forgiveness. We should always seek to understand the other person's position and clarify what was meant by what was said. Beyond that, there may be a need for some honest dialogue to fully resolve such situations of potential offence. Humility is the watchword, and a powerful weapon against the enemy.

A humble, releasing and empowering leadership is a great protection against the enemy's desire to bring people into bondage through a wrong kind of control (what in the past might have been called 'heavy-shepherding'). At the other extreme, the adulation and idolisation of leaders can lead to pride on their part and open the door to deception and exclusivity.

Leadership has many problems of its own - the tendency towards isolation and even deception is ever-present. Without good accountability structures and sound theological input, a 'tin-pot God' leader can quickly devise his own theories and theologies, which suit himself and may bear little resemblance to the truth of scripture. However, many godly leaders who do teach the truth of the Bible are undermined by rebellious people within the church whose agendas are their own and whose end is to promote themselves. They understand little of the protective purpose of spiritual authority and by rebelling against it, in fact place themselves at the devil's mercy. It also has a greatly undermining affect on the unity of the church and the confidence of the leaders.

A leader without vision is no leader

A leader without a vision is no leader. Vision is probably the most essential quality of any church leader. Without it, the people perish, go round in circles and are unrestrained (Prov 29:18[18]). Leaders who are simply in 'maintenance mode' (maintaining the numbers, maintaining the building, maintaining the traditions, etc) are no threat to the devil. He is happy to leave them alone because they are already caught in one of his strategies – maintenance rather than mission.

Churches that once were full of life, without fresh vision will gradually slip into religious rituals, institutional formalities and dead legalism. Our country is littered with such churches. Thankfully, many of them have now closed and new vibrant expressions are emerging, but the danger signs are there for all of us to see. We need to heed the warnings of those who have gone before us. We must beware of becoming old wineskins that cannot contain the new wine. Many 'old wineskin' churches have been split when new wine is brought in through enthusiastic new members. Better to start from scratch and build on a fresh foundation. The enemy loves to get us into dead rituals and meaningless repetitions. These are like the prayers of the hypocrites mentioned in Matthew 23:14[19], which are purely for show. There is no real heart or love for God in these repetitions. Liturgies and rituals can be expressions of true worship, but sadly it's not often the case.

In the absence of true spirituality, some sections of the church have found their reason for existence in doing good works. And whilst God has many good works for us to do, if they're not combined with a passion for the gospel, and a concern for people's eternal welfare then they are simply distracting and fruitless activities. Better a hungry person going to heaven than a well-fed person going to hell (if you find that offensive, just stop and think about it for a moment). The ideal of course is that both expressions of the gospel work hand in hand – the two hands of the gospel.

ARENA 7 - The city and the nation

Ephesians 6 speaks about how the devil works through principalities and powers. A principality is a ruling spirit over a geographical area. I believe these can operate at many levels, from local communities, to cities, and even to nations. We should not be surprised to discover as communities, cities and nations take on particular godless characteristics (e.g. violence, despair, sexual perversion, drug addiction, poverty, materialism, political correctness, corruption, exploitation, a gang culture, or occultism) that ruling spirits are at work and need to be displaced through prayer and action.

The spirit of the age, which is rebelliousness and lawlessness, is prevalent everywhere. In the UK, we see a media that constantly mocks Christianity and undermines the church. How often have you seen a TV soap opera with a positive portrayal of an evangelical Christian?

Our education system, rooted now in humanism, atheism and, more recently, overlaid by a multi-faith agenda, often feeds our children and young people with philosophies in direct contradiction of Biblical truth. Praise God for Christian schools, and Christian teachers, ministries working in schools, Christian Unions, and the prayers of Godly parents. Without this salting effect, I believe our education system would be far worse.

Corrupt businesses buy into the power of mammon and greed, and injustice so often prevails. Exploitation, unrighteous trade, lying and deception show much of the business community to be infiltrated by the enemy - What a challenge to Christians in business and Christian businesses!

Drugs, crime and violence are complicated interrelated issues that are commonplace in all our major cities, and continue to affect Liverpool significantly. Despite the excellent work by drug counsellors, rehabilitation centres and Christian ministries working in this area, the enemy's stronghold through drugs is still great. Young people's lives continue to be destroyed through drugs, violence, and gun crime.

At a national level, I believe that political correctness is one of the greatest strategies of the enemy in our day to silence Christians, to lock up the truth, and to cause conformity towards the liberal elite who are the leaders and influencers in our nation. How long will it

Political correctness is one of the greatest strategies of the enemy

be before our legally- enshrined right to preach the gospel in the streets is removed through fear of offence caused to other faiths? It may be controversial, but how long will it be before parents, who with biblical convictions, lovingly use physical discipline to correct their child's behaviour and instil a sense of respect and obedience, will be prevented from doing so and possibly even be sent to prison? (Prov 13:24[20])

How long before witnessing to a Muslim becomes an illegal activity? How long before Christian foundation schools are forbidden to teach creationism as a theory with equal validity to evolution?

A biblical Christian view of family life has already been badly undermined by laws passed in regard to abortion, divorce and same-sex marriage. Churches who take a stand against same-sex marriage risk in the long term being taken to court for discrimination based on sexual orientation.

Praise God for Christians in Parliament and local government, and for the prayers of the saints, which can hold back this tide of anti-Christian legislation.

Cities can be amazing places to live when there is respect for the individual, the family, and the environment. But pollution, slum housing, and exploitative work places all add to the misery for many.

The spirit of anti-Christ is at work in our nations across the globe. Corrupt governments all over the world make a mockery of the so-called 'public service' motive of those who enter government.

The enemy uses many and every means to hold nations in his grip - May the church stand up and be counted in these days. May it demonstrate the gospel in its powerful acts of social goodness, declare the gospel in full confidence of its life changing truth, and define and claim the spiritual and moral high ground in our nations once again.

4

The weapons of our warfare

We can look at our weapons from a number of perspectives. Let's start by looking at them around our three key sets of relationship / priorities / values. These are Up towards God, In towards each other, and Out towards the world. We can show it like this, first in this bigger overview and then in summary form.

Intercession/ Praise, worship & thanksgiving/ Name of Jesus/ Blood of Jesus – Finished work of Christ/ Believers authority – position in Christ/ Righteousness/ Praying in tongues/ Word of God & Our Confession/ Binding & loosing/ Armour of God/ Renewed Mind/ Power of the Holy Spirit/ Sacrifice, laying down our lives/ Angelic help/ Perseverance &

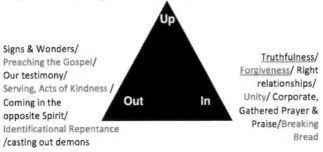

Signs & Wonders/
Preaching the Gospel/
Our testimony/
Serving, Acts of Kindness /
Coming in the
opposite Spirit/
Identificational Repentance
/casting out demons

Truthfulness/
Forgiveness/ Right
relationships/
Unity/ Corporate,
Gathered Prayer &
Praise/Breaking
Bread

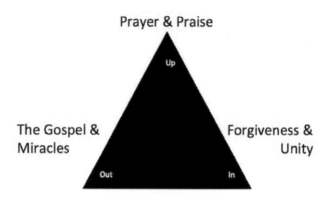

Now lets look in more detail at the weapons in terms of personal, family and corporate weapons

A) Personal weapons

It is often said that the best form of defence is attack. As we look at the following weapons that we use to engage in battle, we will see that some of them are more defensive and some of them are more offensive (attacking). However, the aim is always the same: that we win the battle!

At its most fundamental, there is no doubt that a close, personal walk with God is our greatest protection. It's like walking down the street with a massive bodyguard - No one's going to bother you when they see the size of your protection! Similarly, demons are not going to take their chance when they encounter someone walking close to God, covered in his anointing and ready for battle.

i. Love and forgiveness

We often find ourselves in conflict with those outside the church, in the workplace, the family, in our street, or elsewhere. One of the things Jesus said was that we were to "love our enemies and pray for those who persecute us" (Matt 5:44). These are in fact warfare strategies.

We defeat the darkness not by combating like with like, but by coming against it in an opposite spirit

We defeat the darkness not by combating like with like, but by coming against it in an opposite spirit. Where there is hatred and anger, we must come with love and forgiveness. Paul takes the picture a bit further in Romans 12:20-21 when he says that "if your enemy is hungry, feed him and if he is thirsty, give him a drink, for in so doing you will heap burning coals upon his head. Do not be overcome by evil, but overcome evil with good." Pouring burning coals over our enemies heads sounds like an act of spiritual aggression to me! Let's enjoy watching love win the day.

Walking in forgiveness to others is absolutely vital. Remember how Ephesians 4:27 spoke of the enemy getting a foothold through unforgiveness? We cannot allow "the sun to go down on our anger." Don't let unfinished business drag on to the next day, deal with it as soon as possible.

For years after we moved to Liverpool Jenny was undermined in her confidence and restricted in her freedom to enjoy what we were building in Frontline. It wasn't until she realised she had some issues of unforgiveness from the past and dealt with them, that God released her to enjoy the adventure here.

You need to be able to forgive others whether or not they ask for your forgiveness. When Jesus hung on the cross, He said, "I forgive them for they do not know what they are doing" (Luke 23:34). Forgiveness must be unconditional. For Jenny, she had no control over the other party's response, she just had to forgive. If we wait for others to apologise, we leave the door open to the enemy (and he won't need a second invitation!) Letting unforgiveness hang around in our lives is like living in a high crime area of the city and leaving our back door open all day - It's simply inviting trouble.

However hard it is to forgive others, God will help us to do so, as the following remarkable story testifies (taken from Joyce Meyer's book, *Approval Addiction*):

> During World War 2, Corrie Ten Boom and her sister were held in a horrible concentration camp named Ravensbruck. They saw and suffered terrible torments

including starvation and nakedness in below-freezing weather. Corrie's sister Betsie actually starved to death. During their time there, however, they continually encouraged other prisoners. They kept an attitude of praise and eventually Corrie was released from the concentration camp because of a simple clerical error.

After her release, she travelled worldwide telling of her experiences and the faithfulness of God.

One evening, after preaching in Germany about God's forgiveness and how no sin is too great for God to forgive, she suddenly recognised a man coming toward her. He had been a guard at Ravensbruck and one of the people who had tortured the prisoners. The man did not recognise Corrie, but he said he had heard her mention that she was a prisoner in Ravensbruck. He said, "I was a guard there, but have since gone on to become a Christian. I know God has forgiven me for the terrible things I did, but I am asking you for your forgiveness as well."

Corrie said that she immediately saw her beloved sister slowly starving to death, and felt at that moment even though she needed forgiveness every day herself, she couldn't forgive this man. As she stood in front of him, she knew she must forgive him although she did not know how she could. Everything she preached to others would be worthless if she could not forgive. Corrie said she knew it would have to be an act of the will, because nothing in her emotions wanted to do it.

As she stood there, she told God, "I can lift my hand. I can do that much, but You will have to do the rest. You must supply the feelings." As she woodenly took the man's hand, the power of God came rushing through her entire being. She was then able to say wholeheartedly, "I forgive you, brother! With all my heart, I forgive you." She said that she had never known God's love as intensely as she did at that moment.

Having forgiven others, we are then in a position to fully enjoy, appreciate and benefit from God's forgiveness towards us. When we are living a holy life, there is no room for the enemy to accuse us or condemn us. Repentance over sin and commitment to live for God on a daily basis frustrates the enemy no end. He is unable to get his temptations to take root in us, his accusations to immobilise us, or sin to condemn us. We are totally protected against his accusations. Walking in

His forgiveness is key to staying close to God and free from enemy activity.

It is the foundation of teaching on forgiveness in Ephesians 4:26-27 and 31-32[21] that prepares us for the more obvious teaching on warfare in Ephesians 6.

ii. The armour of God

The classic passage on spiritual warfare is Ephesians 6:10-20[22]. In this passage, Paul encourages us to stand firm against the schemes of the devil. He goes on to talk about taking up the armour of God in verses 14-17. Many people go through a mental exercise each day of putting on each piece of armour. If this helps you to live in the good of the spiritual reality that these symbols represent then that's fine, but perhaps a relevant question would be why ever take the armour off?

The reality is that the armour relates in a large measure to our lifestyles and as such is something that we should be living in the good of all the time. Yes, we may drop our shield or our sword; the belt of truth may temporarily slip from its rightful position, but what is usually needed is a mixture of repentance and renewed commitment to walking in the good of these practices. Simply going through a mental exercise, putting pieces of armour on, doesn't necessarily mean we are living in the good of them.

Truth

Living and speaking truthfully (the "belt of truth" in Ephesians 6:14) means refusing to lie or, as Sir Robert Armstrong once said, "being economical with the truth" (spoken in the Australian 'Spycatcher' trial, 1986). Any kind of untruth is siding with the father of lies (the devil) and giving him access.

However truthfulness is not just about what we say, it's also about what we believe. Are we believing the truth or are we believing lies? This relates not only to one-off and obvious lies but also the heart of our belief system. Do we really believe that God is good? Do we really believe that He loves us, that He is a loving heavenly father who will care for us and provide for us? Do we really believe that we are the apple of His eye and a child of the King? Do we really believe that our life counts for something in His eyes? Do we really believe that He has great plans for us and significant works for us to do for Him?

Holding fast to these truths and speaking out truth denies the enemy access and repels him at the border. This is particularly so when our beliefs in the truths of God's word are coupled with confessions that declare our confidence in what we believe. Try reading these out loud, for example:

"I am a forgiven child of God"
"I am blessed to be a blessing"
"I can overcome every difficulty"
"I am more than a conqueror"
"I have victory in Jesus over fear and doubt and unbelief"
"God will prosper me and give me success"
(scriptures supporting each of these declarations can be found in appendix 2)

With these kinds of confessions, as hard as he may try, the enemy cannot get in on the basis of his lies. It's like we become Teflon-coated to his insidious, undermining lies. They just can't stick!

The belt of truth guards our loins, sometimes referred to as our 'innermost being'. The belt also acts as the place for clothing to be tucked into and when we run into battle, the belt is the place where we attach our sword (i.e. the word).

The word

God's word is a rich source of truth for us to confess. As we take hold of His promises and speak them out it becomes not only a shield of faith to us but also what Ephesians 6 describes as "the sword of the spirit." The word of God in our mouths is a sharp two-edged sword with which we can defeat the enemy, just as Jesus did when He was tempted by Satan in the wilderness (Matt 4:3-11)[23].

Our beliefs and confession about our forgiveness, our salvation, our position in Christ and all the blessings that we have in Christ are like a helmet that protect our minds from so many of the devil's taunting accusations and lies. Ephesians refers to it as the "helmet of salvation" (Eph 6:17).

Righteousness

We believe that we are right with God and can come before His throne of grace without any fear or trepidation. This combined with righteous living is referred to as the "breastplate of righteousness" (Eph 6:14). It guards our heart and vital organs in the chest area. It is a massive protection and means of deliverance from the accusing voice of the enemy. As it is said – when the enemy reminds you of your past, you remind him of his future!

iii. Prayer

Ephesians 6 goes on to speak about prayer (verses 18-19). Prayer must surely be one of the greatest weapons we can use against the devil. Not only can we directly take authority over the enemy through prayer, forbidding him access to our own life and others, but we can also bind his influence over non-Christians as we seek to reach them with the gospel. Wherever we seek to advance God's kingdom, there will be enemy resistance, but Mark 3:27[24] tells us that if we bind the strongman's activity (through prayer), we can then plunder his goods. To bind means to forbid, to veto, to muzzle, or to silence the power or voice of the enemy.

A simple example of such a prayer would be: "Father, in the name of Jesus, I bind the lying spirit that has deceived Tom, I break the power of deception off his life, and release him to know your truth. Amen." Such a prayer does not create instant freedom for Tom, but begins to loosen and weaken the demonic restriction on his life. It opens the way for light to come and for truth to penetrate his mind. Perseverance in prayer, along with loving acts and words of truth are likely to be needed. Ultimately, Tom will still have the freedom to choose for or against God. However, our prayers will help create the environment in which Tom is most likely to choose for God and in which God is most likely to break into Tom's life.

In prayer we can also resist the enemy in the areas of lies, temptation, accusation, discouragement, sickness, doubts, and fears (1 Peter 5:8-9[25]). Using the word of God in prayer is a powerful weapon. It builds our faith and destroys the enemy's lies. We will revisit prayer when we look at corporate weapons of war (see page 121). However. I'd like to introduce you to a recent journey of prayer I've been taken on. I call it the 3C's of prayer.

Some years ago, the Lord spoke clearly to me about my prayer life. It was both an encouragement and a rebuke. I knew there was more and even though I'd been a Christian 45 years, I was still frustrated with certain aspects of my prayer life. I'd have good seasons when it seemed prayer was relatively easy, and others where it just felt like hard work and the motivation to persist in prayer was difficult to find. Sound familiar?

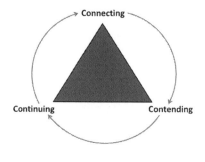

What the Lord said was this:

'Nic you are putting transaction before connection'. In other words I was approaching my prayer times with an idea somewhere in the back of my mind, that it was about getting God to do something for me. If I say or do 'x' then God will do 'y'. That's transaction. What God was wanting was for our relationship to come before the task of prayer. Being very task orientated, this was an easy trap for me to fall into.

So over the next 6 months, pretty much all I did was learn afresh to connect with God in prayer. This often took the form of sung worship, this being the way I primarily connect with God. But it also involved declaring what I knew to be true of God's nature, asking for his forgiveness when needed, rehearsing his promises, and speaking out truth. As I did this day after day, not only did I start to enjoy my times with God, but gradually I learned to discover a consistency in my connection with God. It was what I call a 'visceral' connection. More than emotional, but 'felt' nevertheless.

For the first few months this would take some persistence to get to, often up to 30 minutes of worship and confession. By the end of 6 months, during which time I'd been doing precious little in my prayer times except practice connection, it was pretty quick, often within a few minutes. At this time the Lord said, 'OK Nic, now I want to teach you about contending in prayer'. And so began a season, in which I was learning more of the craft of spiritual warfare in contending for stuff that I knew was on God's heart. This has been ongoing, and still is, some years later.

The final piece of the jigsaw in this rediscovery of prayer was the art of 'continuing' in prayer through the day, through singing, speaking in tongues, praying with others, sending up 'arrow' prayers (like Nehemiah in Ch 2:4 'So I prayed to the God of heaven'), chatting with God about whatever was happening, and stopping for moments to listen to his voice.

These 3C's have revolutionised my enjoyment of prayer, and I'd like to think God's enjoyment of my prayers too! I often find that spending longer in worship, sensitises me as to how to pray for things I am contending for, rather than simply drawing on my natural knowledge, or presumptions of how to pray.

We all connect with God in different ways, your pathway may be different to mine. But my point is this; learn to **connect with God** before seeking to **contend for God** and his kingdom's territory. And then learn to stay connected through the day.

iv.The name of Jesus

Occasionally, someone on staff comes to me and says, "I'm going to meet so-and-so next week. Do you know them? I need to ask them a favour." And I may reply, "Yes I know them quite well actually. When you see them, tell them you're a friend of mine and I'm sure they will do whatever they can to help." This may at times be presumptuous, but it is based on the belief that if they approach this third person using my name as an introduction, then they are more likely to have their requests granted. It's similar when we come to God in prayer. Jesus said that we were to use His name when we asked God for anything and this would guarantee us a positive response

Jesus has been given all authority, so when we use His name we exercise that same

from our heavenly father (John 14:14[26]). It's a bit like the old saying, "It's not what you know, it's who you know." And as we know the Lord Jesus, He encourages us to use His name when we ask for things.

However, it's more than just a polite way of introducing ourselves to our Heavenly father. It is actually taking a weapon of great power into the arena of prayer. The name of Jesus embodies all that He is and especially all of His authority. Jesus speaks about this authority in Matthew 28:18 when He says, "all authority in heaven and on Earth is given to me. Therefore go and make disciples of all nations." Because Jesus has been given all authority, when we use His name, we exercise that same authority. Imagine a policeman stopping you in the street and saying, "In the name of the law, I arrest you." His authority to arrest us at this point does not rest on his physical strength (though that may help), but on two things. Firstly, the uniform he is wearing identifies him as a member of the local constabulary (a little bit like when the enemy sees us clothed in the armour of God). Secondly, he arrests us not by any authority that he has in himself, but on the basis of the authority that the law gives him. When we come to God in prayer, we are able to oppose the enemy's schemes and make our requests in the powerful and authoritative name of Jesus. Time and space do not permit it here, but a detailed study on the name of Jesus would serve us well, strengthen our faith, and increase our authority in prayer.

When Jesus first commissioned His disciples, "He gave them power and authority over all the demons and diseases. He sent them out to proclaim the kingdom of God and to perform healing" (Luke 9:1-2). He gave the same instructions after His resurrection when he said, "these signs will accompany those who have believed in my name. They will cast out demons" (Mark 16:17). Once again, we see the name of Jesus at work and the release of authority over the demonic realm.

I'll never forget one of the first demons I cast out. A younger friend and myself (probably both still in our twenties) had just heard about deliverance and seen one or two demons being cast out. We had recently begun to have some significant input into the local prison in Horfield in Bristol and a young man called Miles came out looking for our help. He described how he would sometimes be overtaken by a great rage and be able to exercise feats of super-human physical strength. When in one of these rages, Miles was known to be able to turn over a car single-handedly. And when the police attempted to arrest him, he apparently sent a dozen or more policemen out of the windows before they finally managed to pin him down.

He now truly wanted to be set free from this power that overcame him on these occasions. As we began to pray, a manifestation took place that reminded us of the Incredible Hulk. It was as though his whole chest began to expand as his face became contorted and his fists clenched. My friend and I thought we were going to be propelled through the nearest window at any moment, or at the very least be smashed to a pulp on the floor.

We continued to pray, rebuking the demon, with increasing disquiet at what was happing in front of us! Just as the manifestation seemed to be reaching a peak it was as though a pin had pricked his balloon and all of the wind went out of his sails (forgive the mixed metaphor). He slumped to the floor with a great sense of relief and his face regained a normal appearance. He knew that he had been set free, and my friend and I knew that we had had a lucky escape! Satan knows whether or not you are aware that you have absolute authority over him. On that day, I think we only *just* knew it!

> *Satan knows whether or not you are aware that you have absolute authority over him*

On another occasion, we were doing some

outreach in the centre of Bristol and one of the team was talking to a young girl about ten yards away by a lamp post. I could see the conversation was getting rather heated and, being responsible for the outreach, went over to see what was going on. In his typical fashion, Jim was provoking the girl with his witness and was quite happy about the fact that she was getting more and more irate. As I began to listen in on the conversation, I realised that she was a witch from a local coven outside of Bristol. She claimed that she was starting to control our outreach with her powers of witchcraft.

As she began talking to me, Jim began speaking in tongues. And the more he spoke in tongues, the more agitated she seemed to get. I also began speaking in tongues and, after a while, she became so agitated that we thought she was going to throw a fit of some sort. Again, just like in Miles' case, there eventually came a moment when she suddenly let out a deep

When the name of Jesus is used in casting out demons, it is a direct hand-to-hand battle of wills between Satan and us

sigh of relief and sagged to the floor, saying, "thank you, thank you, thank you, I'm free!" We happened to be very close to an old Methodist chapel at the time, where John Wesley had once preached. We took the girl into the chapel and were able to lead her to Christ. Once set free from the demon she was able to respond to the gospel.

When the name of Jesus is used in casting out demons, it is a direct hand-to-hand battle of wills between Satan and us. We never need fear demons. Whether they remain silent or manifest themselves in crazy or violent ways we can always take authority over them in the name of Jesus. However, this is not a ritual or formula as is sometimes employed in the practice of exorcism, but it is based on a living relationship with the one whose name we use. When we look at the somewhat comical incident of the Jewish exorcists in Acts 19:13-16[27], we see a situation where they sought to use the name of Jesus without having any relationship with Him. It's fascinating to see that the demons could tell immediately that the exorcists had no real authority. They even tried using Paul's name as a way of accessing the authority of Jesus when they said, "in the name of Jesus **whom Paul preaches**, I command you to come out." The evil spirit merely answered, "I recognise Jesus and I know about Paul, but who are you?" I would have loved to have been a fly on the wall that day. It says the man who had the evil spirit "leapt on them and subdued all of them and overpowered them so that they fled out of that house naked and wounded." - Once again, it's not what you know, it's who you know! The exorcists had the information, but they didn't have the relationship. Let's not be afraid to use the mighty name of Jesus. The more we know Him and the closer our relationship with Him, the more we will be able to access and exercise the authority His name affords.

> *It's not what you know, it's who you know: Let's not be afraid to use Jesus' mighty name*

V. The cross

As we have mentioned previously, the cross of Christ is the basis of our victory over Satan and it is good to remind ourselves and the enemy of that when we are praying. I have a small olivewood carved cross that I often hold in my hand when I'm praying as a simple visual and tactile reminder of the victory that I have in Christ.

vi. The blood

On the cross His blood was shed. In the early days of the Pentecostal movement there was a regular practice of 'pleading the blood'. Often this related to seeking God's protection and personal deliverance. It's a slightly odd phrase and I think at times it was applied more as a religious formula, but there is a great truth in the fact that the blood that Jesus spilled on the cross is the agency through which we find not only forgiveness, but also our victory over the enemy. We can thank God for our forgiveness and deliverance through the blood of Christ.

In casting out demons it's a helpful thing to remind the enemy that it is through the blood he has been defeated. The Jews of the exodus were delivered from death by the blood of a lamb on their doorpost (Heb 11:28 & Ex

12:23[28]), a sign of the great protection and deliverance we have through the blood of Jesus.

vii.   Breaking bread

The blood of Christ is something that we celebrate in breaking bread. In doing this, we remember and we proclaim the victory that we have in Christ through His death. We participate by faith in that victory over the enemy as we break the bread and share the wine together.

Many years ago a team that I had sent on mission to Africa were engaged in some intense spiritual warfare. One of the leaders of the team came under a real oppression and became sick to the point of being delirious. The other members of the team prayed and sought God and finally in desperation broke bread with him. It was in the moment of breaking bread that he was completely set free and healed, and was able to carry on leading the mission as a result.

There are untold resources available to us by faith when we break bread together. Derek Prince and his wife were in the habit of breaking bread together every day to ensure they enjoyed the benefits of all that Christ had won for them through His death and shed blood on the cross. Let's bear this in mind as we break bread in families, in small groups / missional communities, and as a whole church.

viii. Praise

I used to take regular mission teams to the port of Pireus near Athens in Greece and our hosts had an office there that sported a huge painting on the corridor wall. It said very simply: "Victory through praise." I have never forgotten that and have found it to be so true. As we praise and worship God, not only is our faith built up, but the enemy is paralysed. As someone once said, the devil is allergic to our praise and worship. He can't stand

Our praise and worship is the ultimate devil-repellent

being around it. Praising God is the ultimate devil-repellent!

There is a reference to judgement being brought on our enemies as we raise our high praise to God in Psalm 149:6-9: "Let the high praise of God be in their mouth and a two-edged sword in their hand" (remember the sword of the spirit) "to execute vengeance on the nations and punishment on the peoples, to bind their kings with chains and their nobles with fetters of iron, to execute on them the judgement written. This is an honour for all His godly ones. Praise the Lord!"

When Jehoshaphat went out to wage war against the Moabites and the Ammonites, it was the praise of the Levites that caused the Lord to set an ambush against the enemy. This consequently led to the enemy's defeat and the Levites' victory! (2 Chron 20:22[29])

It was as Paul and Silas were sitting in a prison cell chained to the walls singing hymns of praise to God that a great earthquake took place releasing them from their chains and allowing them to get out of the prison (Acts 16:25-34[30]). This also led to the salvation of the Philippian jailor and his whole household – another victory for the Lord initiated by the power of praise!

In 1989, Jenny and I were ministering at a French Christian camp. My sessions were all centred on the theme of 'praise and spiritual warfare.' I began to teach on thanksgiving and kept emphasising how important it was to give thanks in all circumstances.

The next day I had cause to remember my own teaching. We were windsurfing on a nearby lake when I realised that my car keys had fallen out of my pocket and into the lake. I had no spare set with me. While thanking God that He worked all things together for good and helped us in our difficulties, I discovered that there was a Citroen mechanic in the group who were with us by the lakeside. This mechanic

God's power is released through our willingness to thank Him in any and every circumstance

was able to secure our Citroen car by rigging the electrics under the bonnet so that we could leave it there locked. With minutes to spare we reached the nearby Post Office before it shut and were able to make a phone call to our friends who lived a few doors away from us back in the UK. The wife was able to break in, get our spare keys and get them in the post by express delivery just before the bank holiday weekend. The keys arrived the day before we were due to leave. This whole situation tested my willingness to give thanks in all circumstances, and I proved God to be faithful.

There was, however, a greater test to come. After teaching on the power of praise that night, I had a horrendous nightmare where I saw all sorts of body parts and blood and gore. I woke up in a cold sweat, not understanding what was going on and feeling full of fear. As I paced up and down our caravan speaking in tongues and praising God, His peace began to descend over me once more. I went outside to check on the children in their tent and they were fine. The following day I was finishing off a teaching session when there were urgent cries for us to come quickly to the main lobby of the campsite. Something bad had obviously happened.

As we arrived, we discovered one of our daughters had managed to run through a plate glass panel in the lobby, having not seen it. There was blood everywhere. She was cradled in blankets and towels as people tried to stem the flow of blood, and once again I was challenged by my own teaching. Was I going to give thanks and praise to God or was I going to give in to fear and look for someone to blame?

As we drove to the hospital I quietly began to give thanks to God and express my trust in Him. Our daughter had a total of more than eighty stitches in her face, stomach and legs before she was finally put back together. The miracle was that nothing worse had happened. Some of the lacerations were very close to her eyes and vital arteries, but there had been no serious muscle, nerve or blood vessel damage, and eventually all of the wounds healed.

I believe that in both of these situations God's power was released to work through our willingness to thank and trust Him in all circumstances, whether good or bad. We are not thanking God *for* the circumstances but *in* them. Our praise denied the enemy access through fear, frustration or anger and maintained a protective canopy of God's love around us in those difficult moments.

There is an interesting insight as to why praise and worship may have such a dramatic effect on the enemy. In Ezekiel 28:12-14 the king of

"Rejoice always! In everything give thanks for this is the will of God for you"
1 Thessalonians 5:16-18

Tyre is portrayed as a type of Satan, it describes how he was full of wisdom and perfect in beauty: "Every precious stone was your covering... and the gold, the workmanship of your settings (or tambourines) and sockets (or flutes) was in you on the day you were created. You were the anointed cherub who covers" (or guards). This picture of Satan before his fall suggests he was one of the chief angels and one of his main functions may well have been in praise and worship to God, because part of his being was made up of musical instruments. If this was indeed one of Satan's original functions in the presence of God, it would be no surprise if he now found the very sound of that praise and worship abhorrent to him and his demonic hosts. ...So let's get praising! "Rejoice always... in everything give thanks for this is the will of God for you in Christ Jesus" (1 Thes 5:16-18).

ix.Good works

John Wimber used to say he was "too busy doing God's work to fall into temptation or sin." And we've all heard the old saying, "the devil makes work for idle hands." There is obviously truth in these statements. How many of us can think of occasions where we've been bored or tired and ended up watching stuff on screens we should never have watched, or succumbing to other temptations and godless pursuits. There is something about being busy with God's work that forms a very healthy protection against the schemes of the enemy. It not only prevents us from falling into sin, but if we are doing God's work, we are also taking ground from the enemy.

X. Submission to God's authority

Aligned to this is a need to be aligned to God's authority, to be in submission to His will and to be under His Lordship. When we are under His Lordship we are also under his protection. In days of old when there were masters and servants, a good servant, although having no rights of his own, would be afforded the protection of his master. And so it is with us today. When we came to Christ, we surrendered our rights to our own agendas and decided to live for Him alone. Part of the deal is that we get all of His blessings and all of His protection - a good deal in my opinion!

There is however a wider issue of authority, because God delegates his authority on earth. We see this in a number of different contexts. In nations, he invests that authority in governments and local authorities. Romans 13:1-2 says, "Let every person be in subjection to the governing authorities, for there is no authority except from God and those authorities which exist are established by God. Therefore, he who resists authority has opposed the ordinance of God and they who have opposed will receive condemnation upon themselves." That condemnation or judgement comes as we open a door to the enemy by our rebellion. The enemy is quick to take advantage of our lack of protection.

This doesn't mean to say that all authorities are godly authorities. Our experience tells us that is far from the truth. There may be times when we have to disobey such a human authority if to obey would mean disobedience to God. For example, if the laws of the land said that we were not allowed to preach the gospel, then we would have to break those laws in order to be obedient to the great commission. There are plenty of corrupt authorities in the world. What we need to realise however, is that it is not the person or the institution we are submitting to in choosing to do so. It is the authority that comes from God we are submitting to, and in such submission we can therefore be blessed.

Conversely, rebellion against God's authority is viewed very seriously in scripture. In 1 Samuel 15:22-23[31], Saul is rejected by God because of his disobedience and rebellion. The sin of rebellion is in fact likened to divination (or witchcraft).

This God-ordained authority is not solely in the governments of nations and cities, but is also established in the family (through husbands to wives, and parents to children), and in the workplace (through employers to employees) (Eph 5:24, 6:1 & 6:5[32]). This authority is not in order to 'lord it over' others, but is authority to serve, bless, protect and provide for.

God delegates His authority to bless us, protect us and provide for us

Authority obviously also extends to the church (Heb 13:17, 1 Peter 5:5, 1 Tim 5:17[33]). This can be a contentious issue because there is a risk of people being dominated or manipulated by church leaders, as has happened on occasion. But the answer to experiencing (or hearing of) the wrong use of authority is not having no authority, but right authority. If we are in a church where we cannot respect and submit to the leadership and authority of the leaders, then we are probably in the wrong church. Where we find we can do that, it should be a joy and a blessing to know that we are under such protection and blessed by being aligned with God's authority in that context.

Time and time again I have seen people remove themselves from that authority. Some have remained in the church while being rebellious in their hearts or simply choosing to live independently. Others have left the church and remained in that place of isolation. In so many of these situations I have seen people fall prey to the schemes of the enemy (through sickness, the break-up of marriages, financial difficulties etc), simply because they chose to remove themselves from the protection God affords through submission to His authority. Again, God does not delegate His authority to squash us, restrict us or control us, but to bless us, protect us and provide for us.

In the year prior to leaving Bristol, God tested me in many different areas. It was a very difficult year. We knew we were heading off somewhere else but didn't know where. The temptation to have bad attitudes towards others in leadership in the church was great. I knew we couldn't leave without their blessing and I knew we couldn't be blessed unless we kept our attitudes clear. But there was a time when I was beginning to become rebellious and resentful in my attitudes. It was brought home to me forcibly when one of our daughters was nearly knocked over by a car in a nearby street. As soon as it happened, God spoke into my heart and said, "be careful. That's what could happen if rebellion gets into your heart and if my mantel of protection, through the authority of the church, is removed." I tell you, from that moment on I kept my attitude sweet and stayed in submission, despite the conflict that was taking place. God taught me a lesson that day.

Within the church context, authority is further delegated to those who help to care for the flock, to raise up disciples and to train people in leadership and ministry. 1 Corinthians

16:16 says, "be in subjection to such men and to everyone who helps in the work and labours." Church leaders have many helpers within the church, and the same respect and submission needs to be afforded to them as to the main leaders themselves.

In these relationships, clear communication, walking in honesty, quickness to forgive and a willingness on the part of those in authority to continue to be learners themselves will all oil the works. It will ensure they continue to be a blessing to each and every one of us. The enemy will be excluded and God's kingdom will continue to advance. A kingdom, by definition, operates by the king exercising his authority. Without a release of that authority, there can be no extension of his kingdom.

In the context of discipleship, no one should be pressured to do something they don't want to do. But a great way to grow in our faith and ensure we do not allow the devil access to our lives is to voluntarily and willingly make ourselves accountable to those who are helping to disciple us.

We talk about the two discipleship questions – **'What is God saying to me?'** And 'what **am I going to do about it?'** These questions are designed to be low control but high accountability. We do not tell others what to do, but help them to identify what God is saying to them, and then to offer the accountability for them to see through on what they believe they are being asked by God to do in response. This is the complete opposite to the unhealthy, ungodly, toxic, controlling behaviour of some leaders. It is an expression of servant leadership as modelled by Jesus.

xi.Repentance

John the Baptist and Jesus both preached a message of repentance (Matt 3:2 & 4:17), and Peter preached it on the day of Pentecost (Acts 2:38[34]). Repentance itself is a key to victory over the enemy. It breaks the hold of guilt and shame by accessing the forgiveness of God. It strengthens a weak will by aligning it with the will of God, and it awakens the conscience to be far more alert to future temptations. In other words, we become sensitised to sin and start to want to avoid it in future.

Repentance denies the devil access to our lives by removing his legal jurisdiction over us. Satan only ever has a legal right in our lives because of unconfessed sin. Repentance is the spiritual equivalent to a medical 'cure-all' remedy. It touches every area of our lives, bringing us great victory over the enemy. So it is not really surprising that the devil will do everything he can to stop us repenting.

Pride is usually at the root of our unwillingness to repent. Often when Jenny and I are involved in marriage counselling, we come across a situation where one partner refuses to accept blame and responsibility for things they have done wrong. We almost force them to rehearse the words, "I was wrong; I am sorry; please forgive me." When they have said it once, a barrier comes down and it is usually easier the next time.

I have found a similar difficulty with church

leaders. If they make a mistake or do something wrong, they are often reluctant to admit it. It's as though they can't let their image of 'the perfect leader' be tainted by a little bit of good old-fashioned confession. On the many, many occasions I have had to ask the forgiveness of members of the church, I have found it only a positive (if humbling) experience. I believe that love and respect have always grown as a result, not diminished.

Beware of confusing remorse (sorrow) with repentance (a change of heart and mind). It is possible to be sorrowful without being repentant – like Esau, who lost his birthright because of it (Heb 12:17[35]). But there is also a godly sorrow that leads to repentance (2 Cor 7:9-10[36]), which then protects us from suffering the kind of loss that Esau suffered.

Repentance is the antibiotic of choice for the infections of rebellion, pride, selfishness, anger, and

Repentance is the antibiotic for every kind of sin. Keep taking the medicine!

every kind of sin. Keep taking the medicine!

xii.   The gospel

For those of you who are observant, you may have noticed the absence of one crucial piece of armour from earlier in this section. Any guesses? ...That's right it was having our "feet shod with the readiness of the gospel of peace" (Eph 6:15). This means possessing a willingness and a preparedness on our part to share our faith, to share the gospel, and to lead others to Christ.

I remember hearing Brother Andrew, the famous bible smuggler, share about his experiences at border controls in what was the old communist bloc in Europe. Many times, during the cold war era, he would have a cache of Bibles ready to take into an Eastern European country and the border authorities would hold him for hours and hours, either interrogating him or searching his vehicles. One sure-fire way to ensure he didn't get delayed at these borders was to take every opportunity to witness to the guards. If the officers on duty were responsive, they would be sympathetic and if unresponsive, they would not want to hear any more of his testifying to Jesus and would let him through very quickly. For me this is a nice picture of the impact of the gospel on the enemy.

In more general terms, every time we proclaim the gospel, we are taking ground from him. At the end of that warfare passage in Ephesians 6, after speaking of prayer, Paul goes on to speak about his proclamation ofhe gospel: "And pray on my behalf that utterance may be given to me in the opening of my mouth to make known with boldness the mystery of the gospel for which I am an ambassador in chains, that in proclaiming it I may speak boldly as I ought to speak" (verses 19-20). The gospel is obviously the word of God and, as such, part of the sword of the spirit. But there is more to it than that. It is the means by which minds and hearts are won to the

The gospel is the light that breaks through spiritual blindness and turns people towards God

Lord, families are turned to Him, communities are salted, and light is brought to cities. It is the cutting edge of our sword. It is the front line of our infantry. It is the warhead on our exocet missile. There is spiritual 'nuclear power' released as we proclaim the gospel. As Paul said to the Romans, "I am not ashamed of the gospel, for it is the power of God for salvation to everyone who believes" (Rom 1:16).

This power is also demonstrated in signs, wonders, and miracles and they are intended to accompany the preaching of the gospel. As supernatural interventions in the natural order, they are designed to authenticate the gospel message and be a visible demonstration of God's love towards us. They are part of our spiritual warfare, especially when the overcoming of demonic power is involved.

2 Corinthians 4:4 says that "the god of this world has blinded the minds of unbelievers." The gospel is the light that breaks through that spiritual blindness and turns people

towards God. Those who were on course to a lost eternity and hell itself are rescued by the good news, brought into God's kingdom and set on course for heaven. This truly is the plundering of the enemy's house! Reinhard Bonnke calls it "plundering hell to populate heaven." It's the 'go' of the gospel. We should have our shoes of the gospel of peace on our feet at all times, ready to respond to the prompting of the Holy Spirit, look for opportunities to share our faith, invite folks to church and see them come to Christ. Little by little, ground is taken from the enemy and the ultimate battle for lives is won.

Imagine if we equipped each believer to have confidence in three areas – to share their faith story, to talk about Jesus, and to invite people to a time and place where they can explore faith, like an Alpha or Christianity Explored course. It would transform the life of our churches and start to accelerate their growth. We'd see ground consistently being taken from the enemy as individuals and families came to God.

B) Weapons within the family

i. Authority in marriage

We must return to the concept of submission to authority within the family setting because it is so vital if we are to receive God's blessing and stay protected from the schemes of the devil.

A wife will not find it difficult to have a submissive attitude to her husband when her husband is loving her sacrificially as Christ loved the church (Eph 5:25[37]). Such men are worthy of respect. Of course that doesn't mean that the man should make all the decisions, or that he is always right, or that he has any right to boss his wife around and tell her what to do. Both partners will have their areas of gifting and expertise in which they should submit to one another. They should share equally in decision-making and they both have an equal capacity to hear from God in any situation.

But beyond all that, there is an authority that has been given by God to the husband, so that he can exercise due responsibility for the marriage. This authority is to protect and to bless, as is always the case with God's delegated authority. It is not to rule over, to command, to boss, or to dominate. When a wife recognises that authority and has a submissive attitude to it, it provides a great protection against the strategies of the enemy.

Satan understands authority very well. He operates by authority in the kingdom of darkness. Rulers, principalities, powers, world forces of darkness, and spiritual forces of wickedness in heavenly places are mentioned in Ephesians 6:12. And rule, authority, power and dominion are all mentioned in Ephesians 1:21. These scriptures clearly demonstrate that there are different domains of authority within the angelic and demonic realms.

The Roman centurion who came to Jesus asking Him to heal his paralysed servant recognised that Jesus had authority to heal because Jesus himself was a man under authority. He said to Jesus, "Just say the word and my servant will be healed, for I too am a man under authority" (Matt 8:8-9). Like the centurion,

> *To be men and women of authority we, must first be men and women who are under authority*

Satan recognises authority in us when he sees it.

For us to be men and women of authority we, like Jesus, must be men and women under authority. For example, a husband has no right to expect his wife to be submissive if he is not also able to demonstrate that same submissive heart towards others in authority. It is worth noting again that authority is never to 'lord it over', but always to serve. Authority is never taken, it is always given. The more you try to forcibly use your authority over others, the less you have. In that respect, it is like a bar of soap - the more you use it, the less you have.

ii. The authority of parents

The authority of a parent towards their children also provides protection for the children whilst they submit to it. It is not surprising that in today's society there is a great release of rebelliousness and lawlessness amongst teenagers and even younger children. As discussed earlier, the man of lawlessness (the devil) is working to undermine family life. We know that family life provides the stable basis for society and that it is given by God, which is why Satan wants to destroy it. Many parents have completely abdicated their responsibility towards their children and need to lovingly rediscover it.

Isaiah speaks of a day in which God's judgement comes upon the nation of Israel. It sounds very much like the days we are living in, which are characterised by excessive deference to children's rights, rampant rebellion of teenagers, and the general chaos of family's lives. This is quite a fitting description: "Then he will appoint children to rule over them and anarchy will prevail...

young people will rebel against authority and nobodies will sneer at honourable people" (Is 3:4-5 NLT). As children are growing up today with a wholesale disregard and contempt for authority, anarchy in our society is the inevitable result.

A friend of mine who recently started his first year of teaching was trying to deal with some unruly behaviour in the classroom. When challenging the boy, the boy simply replied, "how dare you talk to me like that." The evidence of lack of respect for authority in the classroom only mirrors the lack of respect for authority in the home. The enemy is running amok in our society and the family is a key area where he has gained access.

We must never return to the days of children being seen and not heard, or of children not being loved and nurtured in caring environments. Children should be considered people in their own rights, with rights that need defending, but what we have now is sheer madness. The enemy must surely be rubbing his hands together with glee.

iii. Unity and mission

It is a well-worn cliché, but nevertheless still true that "the family that prays together, stays together." When a family does its best to have some kind of devotional centre with Bible reading and prayer, where a love for God and a desire to serve Him is brought into the heart of the family, then that family will surely be blessed by God.

I well remember my own attempts to do this and often felt large measures of failure at the seeming impossibility of engaging children of different ages simultaneously in spiritual interaction. I don't think it was their fault. It was probably mine. But I do know of plenty of families where a sufficiently creative approach has been taken to make those times fun, engaging and meaningful. Children can benefit so much from seeing the relationship their mum and dad have with God, experiencing answers to prayer as they pray together, and being taught the basics of the Bible (which are so often lost amongst our under-30-year-olds).

Alongside this, some parents attempt to find projects in which the whole family can serve God together. This can also encourage a love for mission and an excitement in seeing what God will do when we trust in Him to work through us. This could be getting involved in a project to help homeless people, raising money for an orphanage, going on mission together, making a play out of a Bible story, or a-hundred-and-one other things. But with mission at the heart of family life, particularly where that mission engages with those less fortunate (in the UK or abroad), children generally grow up with an appropriate valuing of material things and (hopefully) a real love of spiritual things.

For example, one family in the church regularly went on missions to Eastern Europe in a beat-up old ambulance every summer holiday. The children, now grown up, have many tales to tell and great memories to draw on, and I am sure these times were very formative in their spiritual development.

This kind of mission takes the battle straight to the gates of the enemy, not simply waiting to defend our territory, but seeking to plunder his instead. Once again, it bears repeating that attack is the best form of defence!

> *It's worth repeating: attack is the best form of defence*

C) Corporate weapons

Continuing with the theme of authority, godly order in the church (with clear accountability handled by servant-hearted leaders) is a great defence against the enemy and releases people into active service where enemy strongholds can be challenged, territory taken, and people won to Christ. Unity is obviously vital to allow a church to move forward and be an agent for the expanding kingdom of God. A divided and disunited church spends all its time trying to sort itself out internally and fails to connect with the mission that God has for it. Psalm 133 tells us that "where unity is, God commands the blessing" and in Philippians 2:3 Paul encourages the church to be "united in spirit and intent on one purpose." It is impossible to focus on purpose without unity. And the ultimate purpose, of course, is that the devil is defeated so that God's Kingdom cane established!

How much time and emotional energy has been wasted by leaders having to address issues of offence, relational breakdown and divisions in the church. It is some consolation to know that Paul had to deal with the same issues in the church at Corinth (1 Cor Chs 1-4), but this is of little comfort when we find our selves being distracted from the work he has called us to do.

We know from Ps 133 that God blesses our unity with an anointing that we desperately need. Unity provides covering for our backs in the battle. It gives us power in our prayers. It reinforces our family identity from which we are always intended to function. Individualism, as much as division, has robbed us of the blessing of unity, and the power, effectiveness and joy that comes from working from our identity as 'extended families on mission'.

i. Vision

A clear, compelling and uniting vision is a powerful weapon in the hand of church leaders. For Satan to be defeated, it requires a committed, united, sacrificial community of believers. The only way to achieve that is with a compelling vision of what God wants to do. More than one vision is di-vision. The members of the church need to be clear how their passions, gifts and callings, fit into and contribute to the fulfilling of that vision. If a vision is too woolly or too general, then "everyone does what is right in his or her own eyes" (Judges 21:25). It is anarchy. Satan is very happy when everybody is pulling in different directions. No progress is made, and no ground is taken.

That's why it is vital for church leaders to seek God for a clear, compelling and uniting vision for their church. They then need the courage to communicate that to the congregation and invite them to be a part of it. Those who cannot identify with the vision are better off finding a church where they can. No church needs a rebellious internal lobby group working to subvert the direction that the leaders are trying to take it in.

ii. Accountability

One of the blessings for me as a senior pastor in Frontline has been to work with my co-pastor, Dave Connolly. The mutual accountability this provides has kept both of us humble over the many years we have worked together, and, by the grace of God, has given us a stronger and stronger working relationship and unity of heart. Whilst not a structure I could recommend in every situation, when God gives you the privilege of co-labouring with somebody else in a church, ministry, or other type of Christian activity, look for the grace-growing opportunities it will provide and thank God that the responsibility doesn't rest solely on your shoulders. Scripture always teaches a plurality of leadership and this is a real safeguard against domination, control or deception. Different gifts and personalities bring different perspectives, and these will each bring the word of the Lord at different times to help direct the church.

Receiving the wisdom and counsel of other citywide or national leaders, or by being part of a family of churches can also be a safeguard against problems in leadership teams where the enemy seeks to divide through disagreements or personality clashes. This humble, teachable attitude towards outside advisors is a great protection for the church. Whether these advisory relationships are structured (such as within a denominational setting, for example) or informal makes very little difference. It is the desire for accountability and input that is the safeguard, not the structure. For example, an ordained minister could still deliberately and successfully conceal serious sin issues from his superintendent, bishop or 'apostle', whereas an independent church leader could choose to be vulnerable and accountable to a trusted friend in ministry.

iii. Teaching

It is a good idea to teach a practical theology on the demonic and spiritual warfare in main church gatherings and through small groups. This provides a good framework for a dynamic ministry of healing and deliverance in the church. Through this ministry, in small or large gatherings or on a one-to-one basis, demons and strongholds can be challenged, sickness healed, and the devil defeated.

Preaching and teaching God's word is also an act of spiritual warfare in its own right. As the truth is proclaimed, people are set free from the lies of the enemy. And as the gospel is declared, peoples lives are transformed as they move away from the kingdom of darkness and into the kingdom of light (1 Pet 2:9[38]).

iv. Holiness

Maintaining the high level of holiness within the church is essential if the body is to do its job and tackle the forces of darkness. Corporately, as with individuals, the enemy can move right in where there is 'sin in the camp'. After the battle of Jericho in Joshua 6, Joshua forbids the people from taking anything from the looting of the city. Unfortunately, Achan stole and hid some of the spoils. So, because of one man's sin, the army was defeated in the next battle (the battle of Ai). We must teach a standard of holiness and this must be followed through with individuals within our discipleship culture and structures. Otherwise, we may similarly find ourselves unexpectedly defeated.Good works

V. Good works

Just as at a personal level we can overcome evil with good, so we can at a corporate level. We can invade the kingdom of darkness by corporate acts of kindness, loving our community, and being sources of salt and light to it through the various projects and ministries that we undertake. Our very presence in the community through ministries that reach out to the poor and needy - or to those who are bound with the chains of addiction or debt - are a means of invading the darkness and setting the captives free. Jesus proclaimed this was His mission in Luke 4:18[39]. These kinds of ministries not only help set captives free, but shame those who oppress and keep people in a state of bondage or poverty. They also point the way to a gospel that goes hand-in-hand with such acts of corporate kindness.

For a city to be transformed, I believe it is vital for churches to work together (practically) and to work to create a real unity between pastors across the city. This again defeats enemies like pride and sectarianism and releases the blessing of God onto the churches' united corporate ventures (such as Merseyfest in Liverpool in 2005).

The church can also take action at a national level through prayer and by lobbying MPs, gathering signatures on petitions, and generally using whatever means they can to make their political voices heard. Governments won't always listen, but sometimes they will and it could make a massive difference to our communities and nation.

vi.Prayer

A corporate prayer strategy and a praying leadership both multiply the impact of our personal prayer. Jesus promised us in Matthew 18 that

A corporate prayer strategy and a praying leadership multiplies the impact of our personal prayer

where two or three are gathered, there He is in the midst; and if two agree upon anything in prayer, it shall be done for them by their father in heaven. These are clear indications that power and authority against the enemy's schemes are released through united prayer. Prayer needs to happen at every level of church life: small groups, missional communities,, ministries, departments, and as a whole church.

A leadership team that prays together is a

vital protection against the enemy's attacks on the church. Several times in my experience as a leadership we have prayed and asked God to expose sin in the church. He has done it remarkably. And whilst it's been painful to deal with, we've been able to avoid long-term damage to the body as a whole by rooting out sin and helping those caught in its web of deceit to get free.

Corporate prayer practices are many and varied, but I want to highlight a few here that may be helpful

The mixture of high praise and intercession

From Ps 149 we understand that high praise is an important part of our spiritual warfare. What is high praise (the phrase used in the NASB, the NKJ, and the Amplified translations)? The Hebrew literally means the lifting up of God, His exaltation, His arising, and as such suggests a declaration of who he is among us. His majesty, his power, his glory, his kingly nature, his authority, are all part of this declaration.

Intercession simply means standing before God on behalf of another person or situation.

This has two main impacts. Firstly it acknowledges God's rightful place among us, and also over the demonic realm. Secondly it releases faith for us to pray according to our knowledge of who God is among us. As we begin to declare his high praises in song and in our prayers and confessions, an increasing authority rises within us to intercede according to his will for any given situation.

It's important that we pray according to his will, as we know from 1 Jn 5:14-15 that when we pray according to his will 'we know that he hears us, and when we know that he hears us we know that we have the requests made of him.' Wow what a promise.

As we sense the will of God for any situation (not always as easy as it sounds), and start to intercede for it, we know God is hearing and answering our prayers. This done from the place of faith and authority that accompany his high praise, is a powerful basis for our intercession.

James 5:16 in the Classic Amplified translation says 'The earnest heartfelt continued prayer of the righteous man makes tremendous power available, dynamic in its working'. James goes on to describe how Elijah prayed for the rain to stop, and then to restart, according to God's revealed will. His prayers were powerful and effective.

Praying the prophetic

Clearly praying according to God's will is one of the most important aspects of effective prayer. God has given prophecy and prophets to the body of Christ to help us discern the mind of God in specific situations. We need to harness the input of both prophesy (as a gift given spontaneously to anyone in a corporate prayer gathering), and the prophets, to our times of intercession. They will give us laser like precision in our praying which like a laser guided missile increases impact massively.

Paul writes to Timothy in 1 Tim 1:18 referring to the 'prophesies previously made concerning you, that by them you may fight the good fight'. Prophecy like the written word of God is a sword in our hand, with which we can engage in the battle. I know there are several key prophesies that I have received over the years that I regularly refer to in my own times of intercession. Such prophesies are equally powerful in our corporate prayer times. It's good to recall them when we come to pray, as well as being open to new words from God.

The first time a prophet is mentioned in the Bible is in Gen 20:7. Abraham is described as a prophet, and the thing he is called to do in this function is to pray for Abimalech, healing him. The link between prayer and prophecy is marked in the first mention of the prophet. 'The law of first mentions' suggests this is of great significance.

Praying in tongues

The gift of tongues is a gift that keeps on giving. It's used for interpretation in a public setting, edification in a private setting, and worship and prayer in both settings. When we pray in tongues, we can be sure that God understands what is being prayed. As Paul says in Rom 8:27 'He who searches the hearts knows what the mind of the Spirit is, because He intercedes for the saints according to the will of God.' There it is again – praying according to the will of God, a key for answered prayer.

So as we intercede in tongues we know that we are praying according to the will of God, as the Spirit prays through us. It's good to recognise the person or situation that God is putting on our hearts, and then allow the spirit to pray though us using the language of the Spirit for that person or situation.

Tongues sandwich

By this I mean praying alternatively in English (or your native language) and tongues. In 1 Cor 14:15 Paul says 'I shall pray with the spirit and I shall pray with the mind also.' The beauty of this kind of intercession is that it allows us to persevere for quite long periods without running out of steam. We start by identifying what God wants us to pray for, and then start praying in tongues. As we press in to God's presence, we will start to get thoughts and ideas start to come into our mind, or it may be scriptures or pictures. These are likely to be insights as to how the Spirit is praying through us. After a while we can then switch to English and pray out of what the Spirit is showing us. We will do so with considerable faith, as the revelations we will have been receiving will be fuel to our prayer fires. When we have run out of steam in English, we can revert to tongues and start the process all over again. It's amazing how long we can sustain this. It's like an aeroplane being able to refuel in mid-air.

Groanings

Rom 8:26 speaks about the Spirit helping us in our weakness to pray 'as we should'. He goes on to say that the Spirit may intercede for us with groanings too deep for words. This is not something that can be contrived, but is something we can be open to or available for. Earlier on in Rom 8 Paul talks about the whole of creation groaning, and suffering the pains of childbirth. It's clear that our groanings are also like the pangs of labour, bringing something to birth in our intercessions. In 1 Kings 18:42 Elijah is described praying for the rain to come again. He is in the position of childbirth crouching on the ground with his face between his knees. The rain came after some perseverance. One of the OT's greatest intercessors understood intercession as bringing something to birth.

Corporate simultaneous prayer

For most of us our experience of prayer meetings is that one prays while everyone else listens. Not only does this severely limit the amount of praying that can be done, but also it is hard for those not praying to stay focussed. Even if we all add our 'Amen' at the end, it is hardly an efficient way to pray.

There will be times when we want everyone to hear what is being prayed, because it will allow some direction to the corporate praying to be given. It will also allow faith to be stirred in the whole group for something in particular. However the style of prayer developed by the

Korean church where everyone prays simultaneously is a great innovation allowing many more hours of praying to take place in a limited period of time.

Whilst total length of time prayed is no more intrinsically godly than the volume being used in prayer, it does however allow for the release and expression of faith in prayer to be multiplied many times over. In my opinion it should probably be the default type of praying, and the individual praying be for specific reasons only. The judicious use of a microphone to enable the solo prayer to be heard above the noise of everyone else is helpful!

Clearly this type of praying lends itself well to the use of praying in tongues and the tongues sandwich.

The 3 B's x2

Battle, breakthrough and blessing

We all go though seasons of battle, because

as I hope by now it is clear we live in a war zone, and the battle will not finish till Christ the warrior king, the victorious sacrifice, returns to claim us for his own. He will then finally defeat Satan and his hordes, consigning them to the lake of fire (Rev 20:10).

Until that time, because of the cross Satan is rendered powerless / impotent / ineffective, his power is broken (Heb 2:14). God disarmed / stripped the spiritual tyrants of the universe of their sham authority (Col 2:15 The Message version). As Satan continues to roam the earth 'seeking whom he may devour' (1 Pet 5:8) we are on our guard and have been given all the authority and weapons we need to defeat him. We over come him 'by the blood of the lamb and the word of our testimony, and by loving not our lives unto death' (Rev 12:11)

So we go into battle knowing it is only for a season. However those seasons can last a long time, and often before we come through it we are starting to despair things will ever change. In recent episodes where church leader colleagues have battled with false accusation from the authorities, it has taken over 6 months to get to resolution and breakthrough.

When Jenny and I first moved to Liverpool to plant Frontline church we heard of a recent plan by local witches to take out many of the church leaders in the city. The witches had made false accusations about several of the leading lights resulting in them being arrested and put in prison pending court hearings. Thanks to the intervention of Lord David Alton (the local MP at that time) and others, they were eventually released without charge. But those days in the cells must have seemed like an eternity.

When we are in battle mode we need to fight, but the aim is to get to a breakthrough. In the Israeli 6 day war in 1967 they not only took the Sinai peninsular, East Jerusalem and the West Bank, but also the Golan Heights from the Syrians. They employed something called the steel punch. They used all their military hardware to focus on one point to get a breakthrough on the Syrian lines of defense. Once through they could spread out and capture the whole of the Golan Heights.

We also need to put all our strength in prayer, our resources of relationships, our efforts of action into fighting and winning the battle. In those seasons we need to drop other things, which in peacetime would seem totally legitimate activities, but in the heat of battle become distractions. The moment of breakthrough is a time of critical appraisal of what is required. It is a moment for potentially redeploying some of our resources. What will it take to keep the breakthrough going? Where do we need to invest to maximize the result?

Then comes the blessing. The thing we have been contending for now seems in our grasp, and we want to protect it and enjoy it. Some questions that we may want to ask at each stage are on the following diagram.

Battle

Where is the frontline
What are his schemes
What is our strategy

How are we maximising it

How are we protecting it

Blessing

Breakthough

Where is our focus

What are our first-fruits

How are we giving it away

How are we allocating our resources

Binding, breaking, and banishing

As we battle in prayer, the process of binding, breaking and banishing has often helped me give structure to my warfare praying. This can apply to both personal and corporate prayer.

Jesus said we were to bind the strong man before plundering his territory (Mk 3:27). Whilst there may be a number of interpretations of this teaching, understanding how this applies to prayer is a helpful reminder that we have been given the authority to bind / silence / choke off / muzzle the work of the enemy. This obviously requires careful discernment with others to determine where the enemy is at work (and not every difficulty has a demon behind it).

Having bound his power base in the name of Jesus, through the authority given to us by virtue of His victory over Satan at the cross, we are in a position to break his influence on / attachment to / infiltration of us or our situation. This breaking is a definitive statement that we no longer tolerate the enemy's intrusion on our lives.

Having bound him and broken his influence off us we can then banish him in Christ's name. We do not have to worry about where he goes, that is up to the Lord, but we can ensure he is no longer in our environment, family, vicinity or neighbourhood.

All of this is prayed in Christ's name. You may feel more comfortable praying to the Father (as we are taught in the 'Lord's prayer') and so it might sound something like this: 'Father in the name of Jesus I bind the power of the enemy over my finances. I break his hold on my job / bank account / debts, and banish him from my life in the name of Jesus.' Or we may feel confident to pray 'Satan I bind your power over my bank account, I break your hold... etc' If we pray in the latter vein it is very important that we only pray within the jurisdiction that we have been given by the Lord. This is always over our own life; if a husband or wife then also over our family; if a church leader, then over our church; if a businessman or woman then over that part of the business for which we have responsibility. Etc.

All of this is predicated on living a holy life, living in right relationship with our family and spiritual brothers and sisters, hearing from God, and praying under the covering / protection of our church based spiritual authority (those in leadership). If we are operating independently, while living in obvious sin, or at odds with our natural or spiritual family, then we lay ourselves open to enemy counter attack as he has legitimate grounds for his attack (1 Tim 2:8, Eph 4:26-27, 1 Pet 3:7[40]).

When praying within the safeguards of scripture we need have no fear, and can be sure that our prayers are effective. We may not get immediate results but our perseverance will win the day. Lets fight on!

5

The purpose of our warfare

By now you should be starting to understand that warfare affects every area, aspect and moment of our lives. We can never take a holiday from this battle until Jesus returns and Satan is finally destroyed. One of the reasons we chose the name Frontline for our church is because we see that every part of our lives is lived in the context of spiritual battle. It doesn't mean to say that there aren't times of fun, relaxation and rest, but it does mean we can never be off our guard.

The purpose of our warfare can be described in a number of ways. We need to look at God's eternal purpose in wanting to have a people for Himself. We see this right through scripture, beginning with the creation of Adam and Eve and the family that would grow from them. We see it in when God talks to Moses on Mount Sinai and says, "If you will indeed obey my voice and keep my covenant, then you shall be my own possession among all the peoples. For all the Earth is mine, and you shall be to me a kingdom of priests and a holy nation" (Exodus 19:5-6).

God's heart for us, His people, comes through with an even greater sense of His intense love in Deuteronomy 7:6-8: "For you are a holy people to the Lord your God. The Lord your God has chosen you to be a people for his own possession out of all the peoples who are on the face of the earth. The Lord did not set His love on you nor choose you because you were more in number than any of the peoples, for you were the fewest of all peoples, but because the Lord loved you and kept the oath which He swore to your forefathers."

In the New Testament, the same scriptures are quoted in 1 Peter 2:9: "You are a chosen race, a royal priesthood, a holy nation, a people for God's own possession." This is restated in Titus 2:14: "Jesus gave Himself for us that He might redeem us from every lawless deed and purify for Himself a people for His own possession, zealous for good deeds." And the completion of this people is finally seen in Revelation 21:2: "And I saw the holy city, new Jerusalem, coming down out of heaven from God, made ready as a bride adorned for her husband."

God is looking for a bride for his son Jesus. We are in the season of making ourselves ready. God's purpose to have such a people for Himself led to His son giving His life for us. We engage in the battle to prepare ourselves to be such a bride without spot or wrinkle (Ephesians 5:27).

Jesus will not return until His church has realised her full potential, in quality and quantity

So, the purpose of our warfare is to destroy the blight that Satan has put upon the church, freeing it to become the vibrant, dynamic, passionate, spirited bride of Christ.

We live between the first and second coming of Jesus. Our warfare paves the way for Jesus' return. Jesus is coming back for His church and on that great day of judgement, Satan will be finally judged and thrown into the lake of fire. In the meantime, we are called to evangelise the whole earth so that multitudes from every tribe, tongue, people and nation have the opportunity to hear and respond to the gospel (Rev 7:9[41]).

Every person who responds can be integrated to a local community of believers and so be part of God's great army and God's beautiful bride. Hence our old church strap line, 'from neighbours to nations' – We want everyone to have the opportunity to respond to the gospel. No-one need be excluded from the awesome privilege of knowing their heavenly father and being part of God's holy people! Matthew 24[42] tells us that Jesus will not return until this great task is accomplished, and the church has realised her full potential in both quantity and quality.

In this time between spiritual D-day and VE-day, we are told that the whole of creation is groaning (Romans 8:22). Indeed, we can see the effects of the fall and the marring effect of sin on our world in creation itself - Not just in the impact of man through his mis-stewardship of the planet, but also in the natural disorder taking place in the form of earthquakes, famines, droughts, volcanic eruptions, tsunamis, and the like. The good news is this: that creation itself will be set free from its corruption and decay, but not by some random stroke of God's 'magic wand', but by the preparation, maturing, and ultimate revealing of God's people. Romans 8:19-21 says: "For the anxious longing of the creation waits eagerly for the revealing of the sons of God. For the creation was subjected to futility not of its own will, but because of Him who subjected it in hope that the creation itself will be set free from its slavery to corruption into the freedom of the glory of the children of God."

Thus, this people that God is preparing for Himself is not only crucial to the transformation of cities and nations and the evangelising of the whole earth. We are in fact key to the return of Jesus, and are the catalysts that will finally result in the transformation of creation, bringing an end to all its groaning and decay as it transforms into the beauty of God's original intention. The Bible describes this as "a new heaven and a new earth" (Revelation 21:1). God's people will rise to their full stature and creation will seize upon this revealing of the children of

The purpose of our warfare is to destroy the blight Satan has put upon the church, freeing it to become the vibrant, dynamic, passionate bride of Christ!

God in all their glory. Then it (creation) too will be set free and we will be able to spend the rest of eternity in God's presence, doing God's work, enjoying His love and being part of His great family.

Surely this is worth fighting for. This is worth dealing with sin for. This is worth humbling ourselves for. This is worth being trained and discipled for. This is worth sacrificing for.

Rise to the challenge, put on the full armour of God, join yourself to a like-minded community of believers, engage in the process of becoming a mature disciple of Jesus, and let battle commence!

Appendix 1

Scripture references

All scripture references are taken from the New American Standard Bible, unless otherwise stated.

1 Introduction

[1] Revelation 20:10

And the devil who deceived them was thrown into the lake of fire and brimstone, where the beast and the false prophet are also. They will be tormented day and night forever and ever.

[2] Revelation 12:7-9

And there was war in heaven, Michael and his angels waging war with the dragon. The dragon and his angels waged war, and they were not strong enough, and there was no longer a place found for them in heaven. And the great dragon was thrown down, the serpent of old who is called the devil and Satan, who deceives the whole world; he was thrown down to the earth, and his angels were thrown down with him.

3 2 Corinthians 2:10-11

One whom you forgive anything, I forgive also; for indeed what I have forgiven, if I have forgiven anything, I did it for your sakes in the presence of Christ, so that no advantage would be taken of us by Satan, for we are not ignorant of his schemes.

2 The basis of our victory

4 Isaiah 53:4-5

Surely our griefs He Himself bore, And our sorrows He carried;

Yet we ourselves esteemed Him stricken, Smitten of God, and afflicted. But He was pierced through for our transgressions, He was crushed for our iniquities; The chastening for our well-being fell upon

Him, And by His scourging we are healed.

5 John 10:10

"The thief comes only to steal and kill and destroy; I came that they may have life, and have it abundantly."

6 Revelation 20:14
Then death and Hades were thrown into the lake of fire. This is the second death, the lake of fire.

7 James 4:7

Submit therefore to God. Resist the devil and he will flee from you.

3 Primary arenas of warfare

8 James 1:13

Let no one say when he is tempted, "I am being tempted by God," for God cannot be tempted by evil, and He Himself does not tempt anyone.

9 1 Corinthians 7:5

Devote yourselves to prayer and come together again so that Satan will not tempt you because of your lack of self-control.

¹⁰ 2 Corinthians 10:4-5

The weapons of our warfare are not of the flesh, but divinely powerful for the destruction of fortresses. We are destroying speculations and every lofty thing raised up against the knowledge of God, and we are taking every thought captive to the obedience of Christ.

¹¹ Revelation 12:10
The accuser of our brethren has been thrown down, he who accuses them before our God day and night.

¹² Matthew 6:14-15

"If you forgive others for their transgressions, your heavenly Father will also forgive you. But if you do not forgive others, then your Father will not forgive your transgressions."

¹³ Ephesians 4:26-27

Be angry, and yet do not sin. Do not let the sun go down on your anger and do not give the devil an opportunity.

¹⁴ James 1:6-8

But he must ask in faith without any doubting, for the one who doubts is like the surf of the sea, driven and tossed by the wind. For that man ought not to expect that he will receive anything from the Lord, being a double-minded man, unstable in all his ways.

15 2 Timothy 3:6

Among them are those who enter into households and captivate weak women weighed down with sins, led on by various impulses.

16 2 Thessalonians 2:3-7

Let no one in any way deceive you, for it will not come unless the apostasy comes first, and the man of lawlessness is revealed, the son of destruction, who opposes and exalts himself above every so-called god or object of worship, so that he takes his seat in the temple of God, displaying himself as being God. ...For the mystery of lawlessness is already at work.

17 Mark 3:24-25

"If a kingdom is divided against itself, that

kingdom cannot stand. If a house is divided against itself, that house will not be able to stand."

18 Proverbs 29:18

Where there is no vision, the people are unrestrained, but happy is he who keeps the law.

19 Matthew 23:14

"Woe to you, scribes and Pharisees, hypocrites, because you devour widows' houses, and for a pretence you make long prayers; therefore you will receive greater condemnation.

20 Proverbs 13:24

He who withholds his rod hates his son, But he who loves him disciplines him diligently.

21 Ephesians 4:31-32

Let all bitterness and wrath and anger and clamour and slander be put away from you, along with all malice. Be kind to one another, tender-hearted, forgiving each other, just as God in Christ also has forgiven you.

4 The weapons of our warfare

22 Ephesians 6:10-20

Finally, be strong in the Lord and in the strength of His might. Put on the full armour of God, so that you will be able to stand firm against the schemes of the devil.

For our struggle is not against flesh and blood, but against the rulers, against the powers, against the world forces of this darkness, against the spiritual forces of wickedness in the heavenly places.

Therefore, take up the full armour of God, so that you will be able to resist in the evil day, and having done everything, to stand firm.

Stand firm therefore, having girded your loins with truth, and having put on the breastplate of righteousness and having shod your feet with the preparation of the gospel of peace; in addition to all, taking up the shield of faith with which you will be able to extinguish all the flaming arrows of the evil one.

And take the helmet of salvation, and the sword of the Spirit, which is the word of God. With all prayer and petition pray at all times in the Spirit, and with this in view, be on the alert with all perseverance and petition for all the saints, and pray on my behalf, that utterance may be given to me in the opening of my mouth, to make known with boldness the mystery of the gospel, for which I am an ambassador in chains; that in proclaiming it I may speak boldly, as I ought to speak.

23 Matthew 4:3-11

The tempter came and said to Him, "If You are the Son of God, command that these stones become bread." But Jesus answered and said, "It is written, 'Man shall not live on bread alone, but on every word that proceeds out of the mouth of God'."

Then the devil took Him into the holy city and had Him stand on the pinnacle of the temple, and said to Him, "If You are the Son of God, throw Yourself down; for it is written, 'He will command his angels concerning you'; and 'On their hands they will bear you up, so that you will not strike your foot against a stone'." Jesus said to him, "On the other hand, it is written, 'You shall not put the Lord your God to the test'."

Again, the devil took Him to a very high

mountain and showed Him all the kingdoms of the world and their glory and he said to Him, "All these things I will give You, if You fall down and worship me." Then Jesus said to him, "Go, Satan! For it is written, 'You shall worship the Lord your God, and serve Him only'." Then the devil left Him.

24 Mark 3:27

But no one can enter the strong man's house and plunder his property unless he first binds the strong man, and then he will plunder his house.

25 1 Peter 5:8-9

Be of sober spirit; be on the alert. Your adversary, the devil, prowls around like a roaring lion, seeking someone to devour. But resist him, firm in your faith, knowing that the same experiences of suffering are being accomplished by your brethren who are in the world.

26 John 14:14

If you ask Me anything in My name, I will do it.

[27] Acts 19:13-16

But also some of the Jewish exorcists, who went from place to place, attempted to name over those who had the evil spirits the name of the Lord Jesus, saying, "I adjure you by Jesus whom Paul preaches." Seven sons of Sceva, a Jewish chief priest, were doing this.

And the evil spirit answered and said to them, "I recognise Jesus, and I know about Paul, but who are you?"

The man, in whom was the evil spirit, leaped on them and subdued all of them and overpowered them, so that they fled out of that house naked and wounded.

[28] Hebrews 11:28

By faith he kept the Passover and the sprinkling of the blood, so that he who destroyed the firstborn would not touch them.

Exodus 12:23

"For the Lord will pass through to smite the Egyptians; and when He sees the blood on the lintel and on the two doorposts, the Lord will pass over the door and will not allow the destroyer to come in to your houses to smite you.

²⁹ 2 Chronicles 20:22

When they began singing and praising, the LORD set ambushes against the sons of Ammon, Moab and Mount Seir, who had come against Judah; so they were routed.

³⁰ Acts 16:25-26

About midnight Paul and Silas were praying and singing hymns of praise to God, and the prisoners were listening to them. Suddenly there came a great earthquake, so that the foundations of the prison house were shaken; and immediately all the doors were opened and everyone's chains were unfastened.

³¹ 1 Samuel 15:22-23

Samuel said, "Has the LORD as much delight in burnt offerings and sacrifices as in obeying the voice of the LORD? Behold, to obey is better than sacrifice, and to heed than the fat of rams.

"For rebellion is as the sin of divination, and insubordination is as iniquity and

idolatry. Because you have rejected the word of the LORD, He has also rejected you from being king."

³² Ephesians 5:24

But as the church is subject to Christ, so also the wives ought to be to their husbands in everything.

Ephesians 6:1

Children, obey your parents in the Lord, for this is right.

Ephesians 6:5

Slaves, be obedient to those who are your masters according to the flesh, with fear and trembling, in the sincerity of your heart, as to Christ;

³³ Hebrews 13:17

Obey your leaders and submit to them, for they keep watch over your souls as those who will give an account. Let them do this with joy and not with grief, for this would be unprofitable for you.

1 Peter 5:5

You younger men, likewise, be subject to your elders; and all of you, clothe yourselves with humility toward one

another, for God is opposed to the proud
but gives grace to the humble.

1 Timothy 5:17

The elders who rule well are to be
considered worthy of double honour,
especially those who work hard at
preaching and teaching.

34 Matt 3:1-2

John the Baptist came, preaching in the
wilderness of Judea, saying, "Repent, for
the kingdom of heaven is at hand."

Matt 4:17
From that time on Jesus began to preach
and say, "Repent, for the kingdom of
heaven is at hand."

Acts 2:38
Peter said to them, "Repent, and each of
you be baptised in the name of Jesus
Christ for the forgiveness of your sins; and
you will receive the gift of the Holy Spirit.

35 Hebrews 12:17
For you know that even afterwards, when
he desired to inherit the blessing, he was

rejected, for he found no place for repentance, though he sought for it with tears.

36 2 Corinthians 7:9-10

I now rejoice, not that you were made sorrowful, but that you were made sorrowful to the point of repentance; for you were made sorrowful according to the will of God, so that you might not suffer loss in anything through us.

For the sorrow that is according to the will of God produces a repentance without regret, leading to salvation, but the sorrow of the world produces death.

37 Ephesians 5:25
Husbands, love your wives, just as Christ also loved the church and gave Himself up for her.

38 1 Peter 2:9

But you are a chosen race, a royal priesthood, a holy nation, a people for God's own possession, so that you may proclaim the excellencies of Him who has called you out of darkness into His marvellous light;

39 Luke 4:18

"The spirit of the Lord is upon me, because he has anointed me to preach the gospel to the poor. He has sent me to proclaim release to the captives, and recovery of sight to the blind, to set free those that are oppressed."

[40] 1 Timothy 2: 8

Therefore I want the men in every place to pray, lifting up holy hands, without wrath or dissension.

Ephesians 4: 26 -27

Be angry, and yet do not sin; do not let the sun go down on your anger, and do not give the devil an opportunity.

1 Peter 3:7

You husbands in the same way, live with your wives in an understanding way, as with someone weaker, since she is a woman; and show her honour as a fellow heir of the grace of life, so that your prayers will not be hindered.

5 The purpose of our warfare

[41] Revelation 7:9
After these things I looked, and behold, a great multitude which no one could count, from every nation and all tribes and peoples and tongues, standing before the throne and before the Lamb, clothed in white robes, and palm branches were in their hands;

42 Matthew 24:14
This gospel of the kingdom shall be preached in the whole world as a testimony to all the nations, and then the end will come.

Appendix 2

Positive declarations

Declare God's truth daily. If you struggle to accept what God says about you, look up these scriptures and start speaking them out loud every day alongside your positive confessions.

I am a forgiven child of God

   1 John 3:10

   1 John 2:12

   Acts 10:43

   Acts 13:38-39

   Ephesians 1:7

I am blessed to be a blessing

   Genesis 12:2-3

I can overcome every difficulty; I am more than a conqueror

   Romans 8:37

I have victory in Jesus over fear and doubt
and unbelief

    1 Corinthians 15:57

    2 Timothy 1:7

God will prosper me and give me success

    Jeremiah 29:11

40892637R00092

Printed in Poland
by Amazon Fulfillment
Poland Sp. z o.o., Wrocław